Story Play

STORY PLAY
Costumes, Cooking, Music, and More
for Young Children

Joyce Harlow

1992
TEACHER IDEAS PRESS
A Division of
Libraries Unlimited, Inc.
Englewood, Colorado

TEACHER IDEAS PRESS
A Division of
Libraries Unlimited, Inc.
P.O. Box 6633
Englewood, Colorado 80155-6633

Library of Congress Cataloging-in-Publication Data

Harlow, Joyce.
    Story play : costumes, cooking, music, and more for young children
/ Joyce Harlow.
    xii, 202 p.   22x28 cm.
    Includes bibliographical references and index.
    ISBN 1-56308-037-0
    1. Drama in education. 2. College and school drama. I. Title.
PN3171.H27 1992
371.3'32--dc20   92-31800
                                                                      CIP

Dedicated with love to
my mother,
Gladys Durbin,
singer of my first nursery rhymes,
my brothers and sisters,
Roger, Lawrence, Deanna, Joan, Daniel, Deborah, and Barbara,
co-conspirators of childhood fantasies,
my daughters,
Victoria and Pamela,
believers in fairy tales and dreams come true,
my husband,
Richard,
giver of space and freedom to be me, the best gift of all.

A special acknowledgement to
the teachers and students of Summerfield Academy,
without whom this book would not have been possible.

Most importantly of all,
Joyce Armstrong Carroll and Edward Wilson
for their special friendship, encouragement, and support.

CONTENTS

INTRODUCTION

THE FAIRY-TALE THEMES

Each fairy-tale theme in *Story Play* is designed to integrate literature with dramatic play, reading, writing, art, cooking, math, science, music, and cooperative group experiences. Each experience is designed to be child initiated and developmentally appropriate for whatever age level it is used. The book is designed to be used as a whole curriculum or used in parts to complement an existing program. Each thematic unit can last from two to three weeks depending upon the teacher and the students. The teacher sets the stage and then becomes the facilitator of the learning process. The stage is set with the introduction of the fairy-tale theme through the literature. The costumes, masks, play props, and puppets start the experiences.

The "Drama/Play Experience" is introduced through simpletees costumes (see page 2) made in advance by the teacher. The face masks and stick puppets can be made by the teacher or by the children. They are designed with minimal illustrated features, allowing the children more freedom for their own interpretations of the characters.

The "Literature/Writing Experience" uses many different versions of the fairy tales. After experiencing the stories and the drama play the children write their own versions of the fairy tale. This is a group activity with the children dictating the story to the teacher. The story is written on a large sheet of chart paper. The teacher can play word games with the story by asking if anyone can find a word that they know. The children then play with the story and read it themselves or read it to a friend. The teacher may provide a small pointer for them to use.

The key-word books are prepared in advance by the teacher. Each book measures 3 by 6 inches with approximately five sheets of paper between the covers. The sheets of paper inside are unlined to allow for the development of fine motor skills. The key words are written on word cards and placed in a writing center for an independent activity. The teacher introduces the words by writing and verbalizing each word as he or she places them in a basket or pocket chart. The children repeat the word, and then word games can be played by the teacher and the children. The children play the word game with each other as an open-ended activity. The key words can then be used with the shape book developed for each theme. The shape book allows the children to become authors and illustrators of their own books. The children can trace the covers from templates on white pages precut by the teacher. The books are stapled together with as many pages as the teacher feels is appropriate for the students. The key words allow the children to choose the writing to go with their illustrations and are completely open-ended for individual differences.

The "Cooperative/Group Experience" designed for each fairy-tale theme fosters social acceptance, interaction, and problem solving as a whole. Parents are often involved in this process by contributing the needed materials.

The "Art/Writing Experience" always includes a tempera or watercolor painting to go with the fairy-tale theme. The paintings lend themselves to a written caption and can be bound together for a classroom book and placed in the book center.

The "Cooking/Math Experience" naturally introduces beginning math concepts and skills. Each fairy-tale theme uses a simple rebus recipe for an independent cooking activity with very little teacher interaction.

The "Science/Discovery Experience" includes scientific facts wherever they can be brought in. A picture gallery is included whenever possible. *National Geographic Magazine* can provide many real-life animal pictures. Whenever possible plastic animals may be added to the block center for added integration of the theme.

The "Music/Poetry/Game Experience" was the most challenging part of the book for me to write. It was difficult to locate and find music to accompany the experiences. I approached Pamela Copus with my problem, and together we designed the original music to go with the 10 fairy-tale themes. The music sets the book apart and provides the unifying element to the whole concept of the experiences. Alternative experiences are suggested for use without the tape.

The name *simpletees* describes the basic concept of the costumes designed for each fairy-tale theme. The base of all the costumes is an extra-large short-sleeved T-shirt. These are the easiest for the children to pull on over their clothing. Felt and fake fur are used with the costumes because they require no finished edges. A hot glue gun is used to attach the pieces to the costume. Cardboard should be slipped inside the T-shirt to prevent the T-shirt from sticking together. A craft stick can be used to press the fabric into the hot glue. Rips and tears can easily be mended with the hot glue. Because the glue gun reaches high temperatures, the teacher should make the costumes in advance. Because each thematic unit is designed to last only two or three weeks, the costumes receive minimal wear and tear. The T-shirts with lace ruffles can be used for any female character. One wolf costume takes care of all your wolf needs. Hang the costumes when not in use to eliminate wrinkles. Each chapter includes instructions for constructing the basic costumes. Teachers who wish to make more elaborate costumes may consult the section "Supplementary Costume Pieces," which is included near the end of most chapters. The simpletees are fun to make and can be shared with other teachers.

CHAPTER 1

LITTLE RED RIDING HOOD

DRAMA/PLAY EXPERIENCE

Set the stage for the introduction of "Little Red Riding Hood" by reading the story. An excellent one to start with is James Marshall's version, which features a granny who loves to read. (See bibliography, page 22.) Introduce and demonstrate the simpletees costumes and props.

Simpletees Costumes

Use simpletees costumes of Red Riding Hood, the wolf, the grandmother, and the woodsman for a dramatic play experience. (See figure 1.1.)

Play Props

Play props can include a small picnic basket with a tea set and play food. A small quilt can serve as the grandmother's bed. Include a satin sleep cap and fluffy house slippers. Add a plastic, foam rubber, or cardboard ax. (Halloween is a good time to find plastic or foam rubber axes.)

Face Masks

Create face masks of Red Riding Hood, the grandmother, the wolf, and the woodsman. (See figures 1.2, 1.3, 1.4, and 1.5.) Use tagboard templates to create the individual masks.

Stick Puppets/Paper Bag Theater

Make stick puppets of Red Riding Hood, the wolf, the grandmother, and the woodsman. (See figure 1.6.) Create a paper bag theater for the stick puppets. (See figure 1.7.) Present the play to a friend or take home to present to parents.

Woodsman Experience

Use a stump or log of wood, roofing nails (short nails with large heads), small hammers, a toolbox, a nail apron, safety goggles, and hard hats for a woodsman's experience. Place the stump or log on a sturdy piece of plastic and hammer the nails into the wood. Wear a simpletees woodsman's costume.

Fig. 1.1. Simpletees costumes: Little Red Riding Hood.

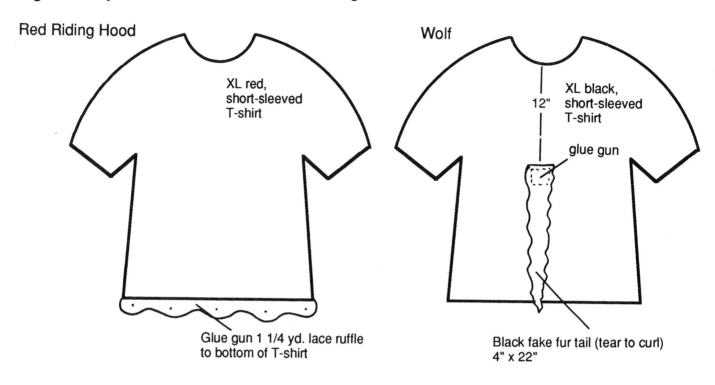

Red Riding Hood

XL red,
short-sleeved
T-shirt

Glue gun 1 1/4 yd. lace ruffle
to bottom of T-shirt

Wolf

12"

XL black,
short-sleeved
T-shirt

glue gun

Black fake fur tail (tear to curl)
4" x 22"

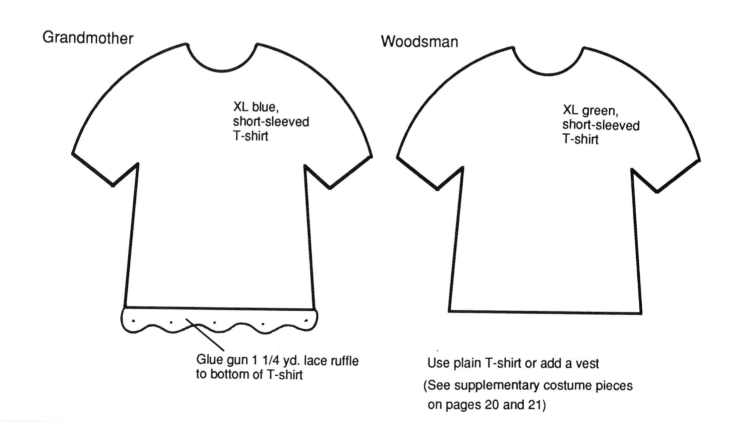

Grandmother

XL blue,
short-sleeved
T-shirt

Glue gun 1 1/4 yd. lace ruffle
to bottom of T-shirt

Woodsman

XL green,
short-sleeved
T-shirt

Use plain T-shirt or add a vest

(See supplementary costume pieces
on pages 20 and 21)

Fig. 1.2. Little Red Riding Hood face mask pattern.

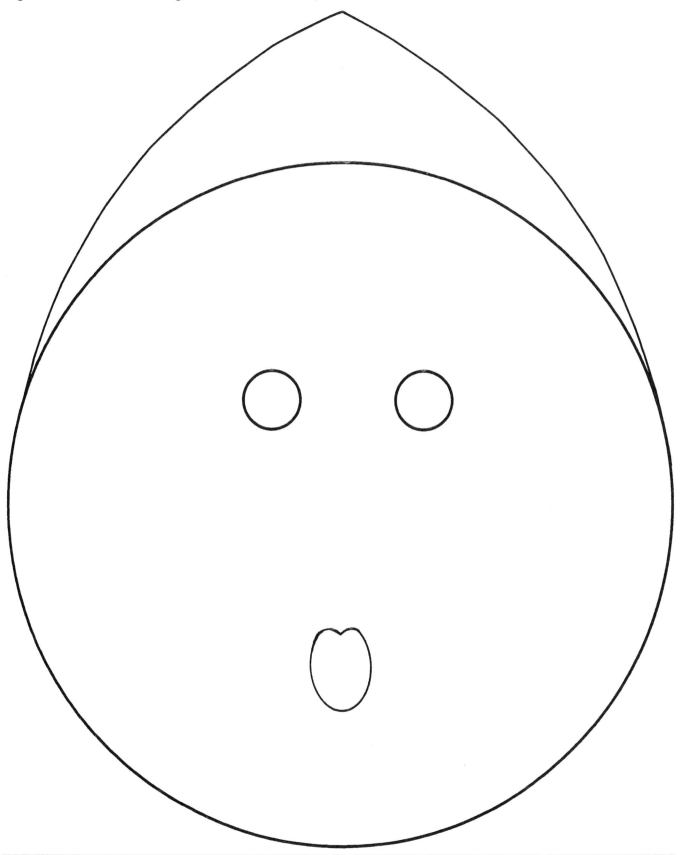

Fig. 1.3. Grandmother face mask pattern.

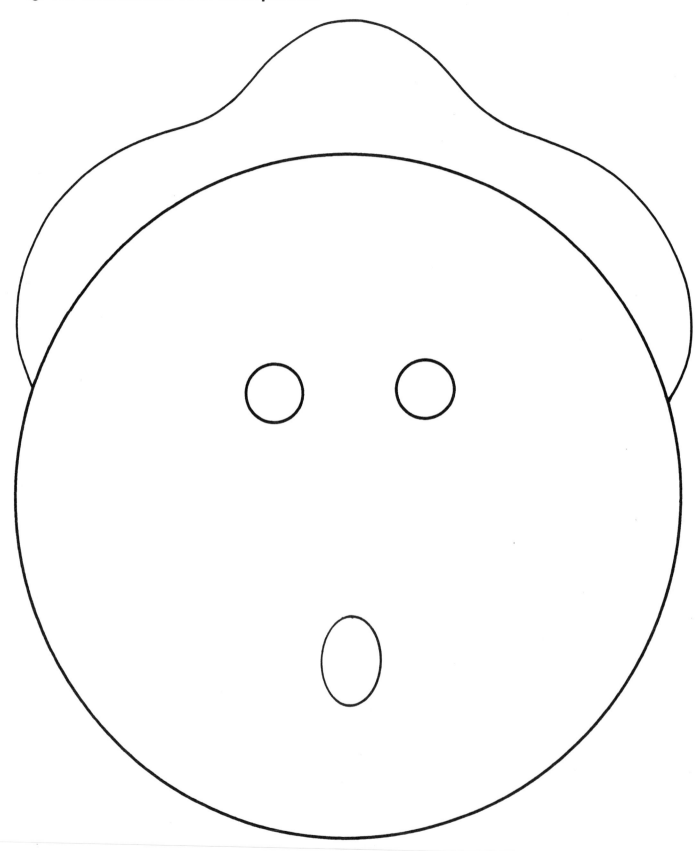

Fig. 1.4. Wolf face mask pattern.

Fig. 1.5. Woodsman face mask pattern.

Fig. 1.6. Little Red Riding Hood stick puppet patterns.

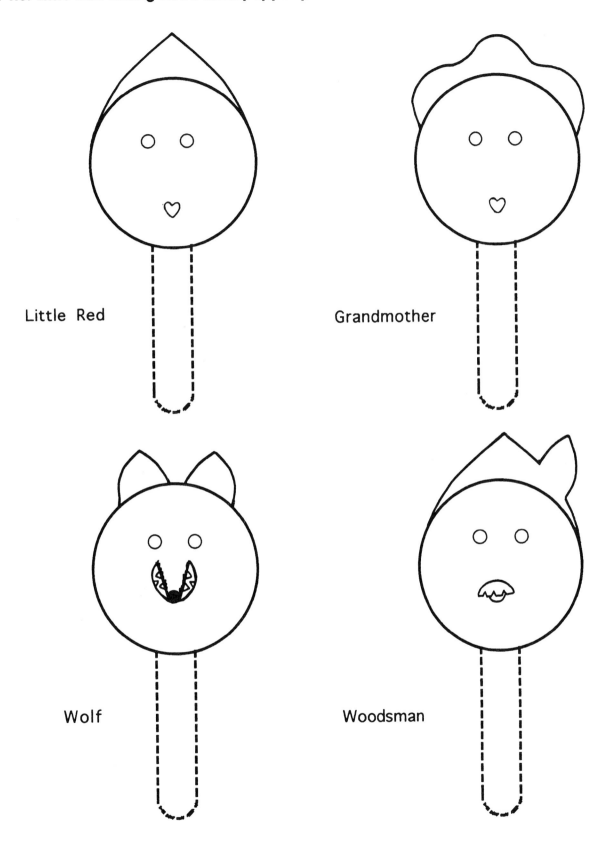

Little Red

Grandmother

Wolf

Woodsman

Fig. 1.7. Paper bag puppet theater.

Materials:

Small paper bag
Markers
Scissors
Stapler

What to Do:

Push out sides of bag and flatten.

Cut opening through both front and back of bag (allows puppets to show through).

Fold excess length of bag inside.

Staple inside to strengthen sides.

Decorate with markers.

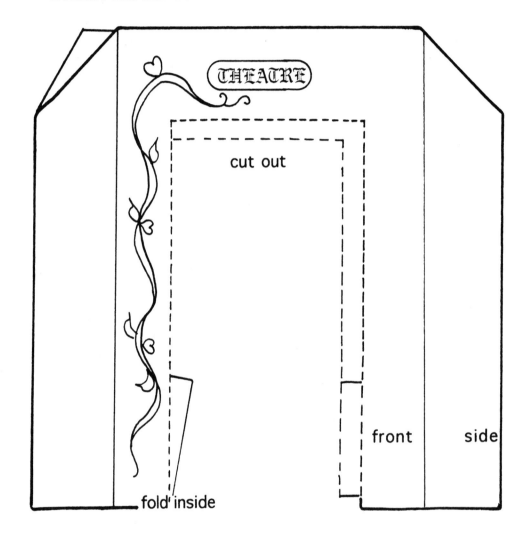

LITERATURE/WRITING EXPERIENCE

Little Red Riding Hood *Versions*

Read and discover how versions of "Little Red Riding Hood" differ from each other. (See bibliography, page 22.) For example, in John S. Goodall's version, Red Riding Hood is a mouse, and there are no words. Cooper Edens's version is illustrated from a variety of old books. Beni Montresor shows Red Riding Hood in the stomach of the wolf and then leaves the ending to the imagination of the reader. Explore and discuss how this version might end. Write or illustrate the ending, or do both.

Little Red Riding Hood *Children's Version*

Write a children's version of "Little Red Riding Hood" after reading and sharing the different stories. Let the children decide upon the characters and ending to their version of "Little Red Riding Hood."

Key-Word Books and Key Words

Make a key-word book using the unique or important words in the story. The key words for "Little Red Riding Hood" are as follows:

Little	Red	Riding
Hood	wolf	grandmother
woodsman	wood	path
forest	latch	

Red Riding Hood Shape Book

Make a Red Riding Hood shape book from tagboard templates. (See figure 1.8.) Illustrate the book and write the story or dictate it to the teacher. Use key words for an independent writing experience.

Wolf Lift-the-Flap Book

Make a lift-the-flap book about the wolf. (See figure 1.9.) Illustrate what might be in a wolf's tummy. Younger children can glue small stones inside the flap. Complete the sentence "Inside my wolf's tummy I put _____!"

Special Grandmother

Read *Grandma's Bill* by Martin Waddell. A little boy's grandmother remembers life with his grandfather, Bill, from a photograph album. The little boy's name also is Bill. Bring an article from home that represents your grandmother. Discuss how each grandmother is special. Read *Kevin's Grandma* by Barbara Williams and *With Love from Gran* by Dick Gackenbach. (See bibliography, page 22, for these and other books.) Display the grandmother articles.

Fig. 1.8. Little Red Riding Hood shape book directions and pattern.

Materials:

Red construction paper
Tagboard template
White paper
Markers or crayons
Scissors
Stapler
Key words

What to Do:

Using tagboard template, trace and cut 2 Red Riding Hood shapes from red construction paper.

Teacher may precut white pages.

Staple the cover and pages together.

Illustrate the book with markers or crayons.

Write the story or dictate it to the teacher.

Use key words for an independent writing experience.

Fig. 1.8.—*Continued.*

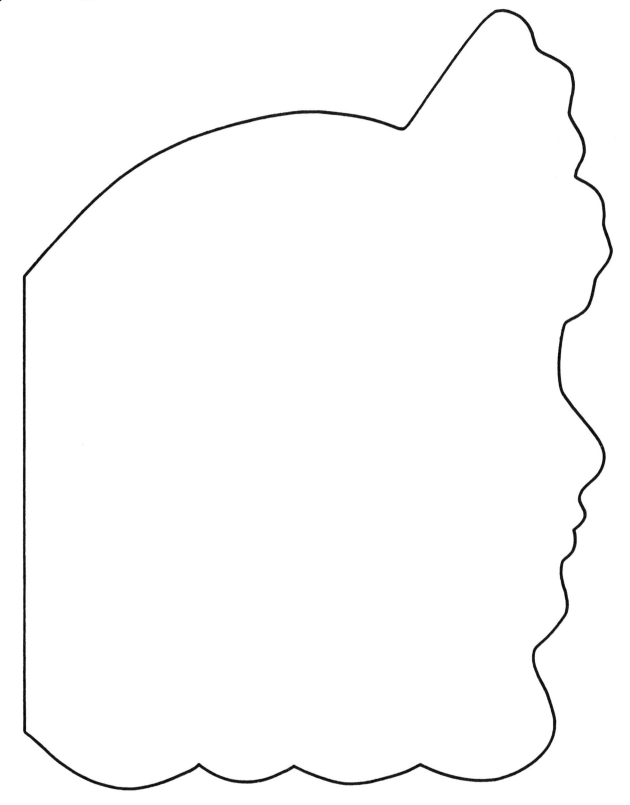

Fig. 1.9. Wolf lift-the-flap book and pattern.

Materials:

Gray construction paper
Tagboard template
Markers or pencils
Scissors
Small stones

What to Do:

Fold construction paper in half.

Trace tagboard wolf pattern on one half of gray paper and cut out.

Cut out flap for tummy on top side.

Glue outside edges together. Only the flap will lift up.

Draw the wolf's face.

Glue stones inside your wolf's tummy.

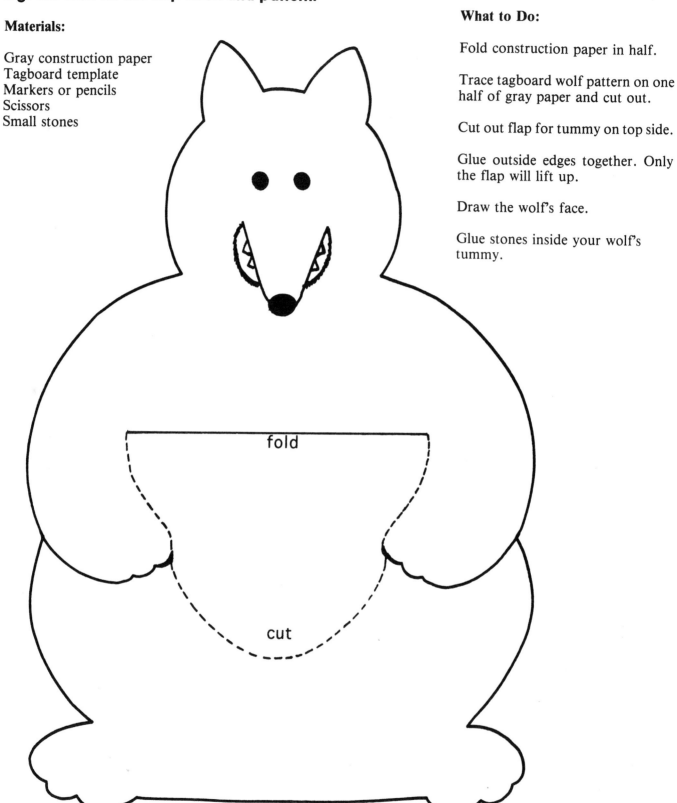

COOPERATIVE/GROUP EXPERIENCE

Grandmother's Cottage

Make grandmother's cottage from a large cardboard box. Purchase a wardrobe box from a moving company. Open the box at the seam and turn the box inside out for a blank surface to paint on. Paint the cottage with tempera paints. Make a roof with the top flaps of the box so that the cottage will be all one piece. Seal the box with paper sealing tape or a glue gun.

Wolf Trap

Read Michele Lemieux's version of *Peter and the Wolf*, a story about a little boy who captures a wolf. Bring small boxes, paper tubes, berry baskets, spools, or other interesting articles, from home. Use a large cardboard box for the base and glue the articles on it to make a wolf trap. Paint the trap black so the wolf can't see it at night. Set the trap outside overnight to trap a wolf. Use a wolf cookie for the bait. (See Cooking/Math Experience, page 15.)

ART/WRITING EXPERIENCE

Tempera Paintings

Paint a tempera picture of Little Red Riding Hood and the wolf. Write or dictate a sentence or story about the picture. Display the paintings on the walls or the bulletin board. Bind the paintings together to make a classroom book.

Monoprint Wolf

Use black tempera in a squeeze bottle to make a monoprint wolf. Squeeze a small amount of black tempera on a flat tray or other smooth surface. Lay a sheet of 6-by-7-inch paper over the blob of paint. Rub the back of the paper with hands or fingertips until the paint has spread out. Lift the paper off to reveal the imaginary monoprint wolf. Write a caption under each wolf or complete the sentence "If I saw a wolf in my bed I would _____!" Children will complete the sentence, and younger children can dictate their sentence to the teacher. Bind the prints together to make a classroom book. Use the wolf-shaped pattern for the book cover. (See figure 1.10.)

Fig. 1.10. Wolf book cover pattern.

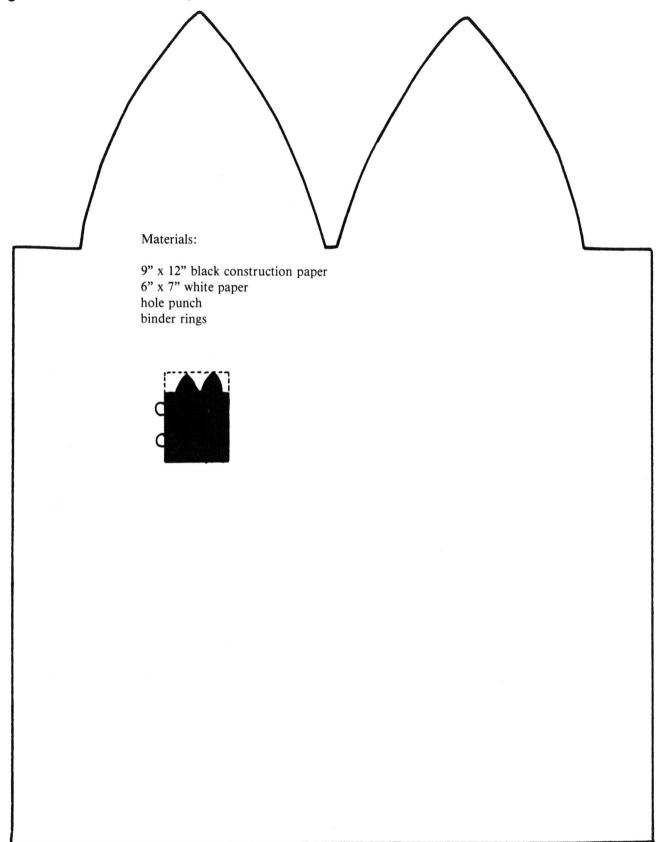

Materials:

9" x 12" black construction paper
6" x 7" white paper
hole punch
binder rings

COOKING/MATH EXPERIENCE

Stone Cookies

Bake cookies for a group cooking experience. Use the rebus recipe to discuss measurements of teaspoon and cup. (See figure 1.11.) Determine how many "stones" will go into each cookie.

Wolf Cookies

Bake wolf cookies. Use a basic sugar cookie recipe or purchase prepared cookie dough. Roll out the dough and use a wolf cookie cutter (a coyote or dog cookie cutter may also be used). Bake, cool, and ice the cookies with chocolate or black icing. Use one cookie as bait for the wolf trap.

Fig. 1.12. Wolf sponge-stamp pattern.

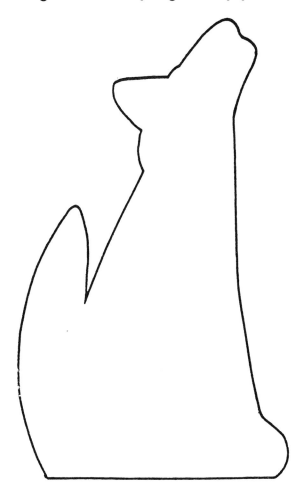

Sponge-Stamp Wolves

Trace and cut out the wolf pattern on compressed sponge sheets. (See figure 1.12.) Sponge-stamp wolves on a sheet of paper. Count the wolves and write the number on the paper. Circle groups of wolves to form sets. Combine the sets on a simple bar graph and discuss the differences.

SCIENCE/DISCOVERY EXPERIENCE

Wolf Facts

Find out about wolves. Read *ZOOBOOKS Wolves* by John Bonnett Wexco. A wolf looks like a large German shepherd with a long, bushy tail and short ears that stand straight up. Wolves mate for life and live together in groups or packs. The female will have a litter of 4 to 14 pups. Wolf babies are born in a den that is dug under the ground. Both parents train the pups and supply them with food. A wolf has five toes on each front foot and four on each rear foot. A wolf runs on his toes. Wolves howl to communicate with each other and also to gather the pack together before a hunt.

Picture Gallery

Display pictures of real wolves. An excellent source for pictures is *National Geographic Magazine*.

Plastic Wolves

Purchase plastic wolves from nature catalogs or from school supply stores. Add plastic wolves to the block center. Safari, Ltd., is an excellent source for authentic reproductions of animal and sea life. Write for a catalog. (See bibliography on page 24.)

Fig. 1.11. Stone Cookies.

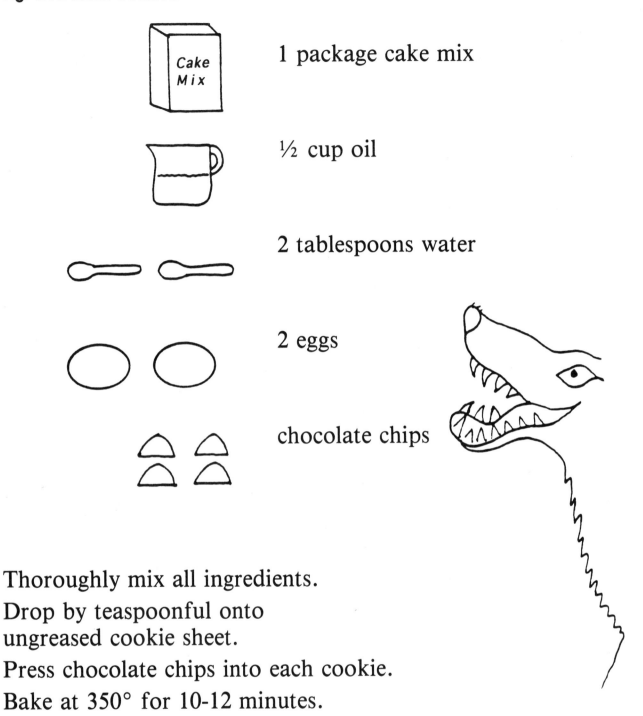

1 package cake mix

½ cup oil

2 tablespoons water

2 eggs

chocolate chips

Thoroughly mix all ingredients.
Drop by teaspoonful onto
ungreased cookie sheet.
Press chocolate chips into each cookie.
Bake at 350° for 10-12 minutes.

MUSIC/POETRY/GAME EXPERIENCE

The Gunniwolf

In *The Gunniwolf*, edited by Wilhelminia Harper, a little girl meets the Gunniwolf when she forgets her mother's warning not to venture into the jungle. Divide the class in half with one side becoming the "pitty-pats" and the other side becoming the "hunker-chas." The "pitty-pat" sound can be made by patting the thighs. The "hunker-cha" sound can be voiced and accompanied by a rowing motion with the arms. If enough room is available, the children can do a tiptoe run for the "pitty-pats" and a leaping motion for the "hunker-chas." "The Gunniwolf" experience can take place on the floor or in chairs.

Rhythm instruments may also be used. Bells or cymbols can be used for the "pitty-pats." Drums or rhythm sticks can be used for the "hunker-chas."

"The Gunnywolf," a musical fantasy performed by Pamela Copus, may be used to accompany the above experience. (See bibliography on page 24.) The music simulates the "pitty-pat" sound of the little girl running with the "hunker-cha" sound of the wolf in pursuit.

The Wolf Went Over the Mountain

Sing "The Bear Went Over the Mountain" (traditional) and substitute *wolf* for *bear*.

Oh, the wolf went over the mountain,

The wolf went over the mountain,

The wolf went over the mountain

To see what he could see.

And all that he could see,

And all that he could see

Was the other side of the mountain,

The other side of the mountain,

The other side of the mountain

Was all that he could see.

SUPPLEMENTARY COSTUME PIECES

Supplementary costume pieces are in figures 1.13, 1.14, 1.15, and 1.16.

Fig. 1.13. Red Riding Hood costume.

Materials:

1 yard of red craft felt
1 red 42" shoelace
Scissors
Glue gun

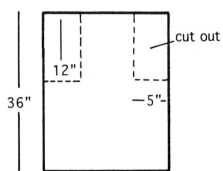

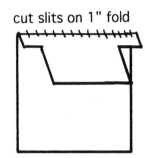

cut out

cut slits on 1" fold

30"

Construction:

• Cut a 30" x 36" rectangle of red felt.

• Cut out 2 5" x 12" pieces from top of rectangle (see illustration).

• Make a fold 13½" from the top and cut tiny slits 1" apart across the fold (see illustration).

• Fold hood in half lengthwise and glue gun top seam together.

• Let glue dry and then turn hood inside out to hide seam.

• Insert shoelace in slits and gather.

• Center shoelace and glue gun to edge of felt to prevent slipping.

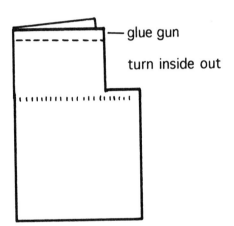

glue gun

turn inside out

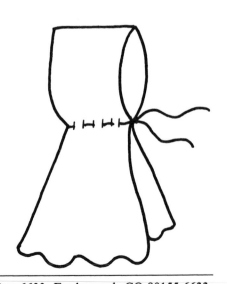

Fig. 1.14. Wolf ears.

Materials:

⅛ yard of black craft felt
4" strip of Velcro™ Sticky Back
    tape, ¾" wide
Scissors
Glue gun

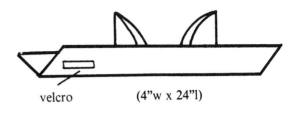

velcro   (4"w x 24"l)

Construction:

- Use pattern to cut 2 black felt wolf ears.

- Cut a 4" x 26" strip of black felt for headband.

- Fold headband in half and pin in place.

- Fold ears in half and glue gun inside headband (see illustration).

- Glue gun headband together.

- Glue gun Velcro strips to ends of headband.

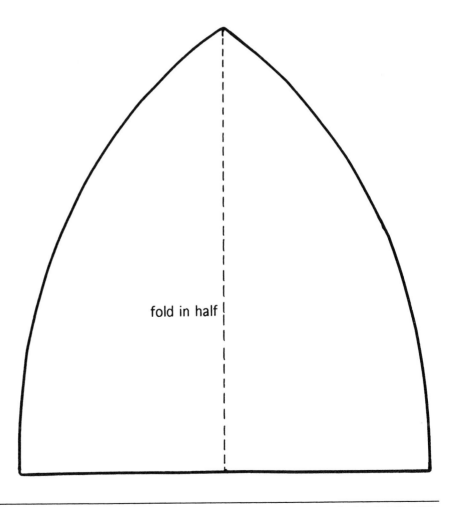

fold in half

Fig. 1.15. Woodsman's vest.

Materials:

½ yd. of green, brown, or blue craft felt
1 42" yellow shoelace
Scissors
Glue gun

Construction:

- Cut a 20" x 48" rectangle of felt in half lengthwise.

- Fold rectangle in half lengthwise.

- Fold in half again crosswise and cut a 6" V-shaped neck opening (see illustration).

- Cut 3" neck opening on front of vest (see illustration).

- Cut 4 slits on each side of front neck opening (see illustration).

- Thread shoelace through slits and tie.

- Starting 10" from the top glue gun a seam on each side to make armhole openings.

- Wear vest over T-shirt.

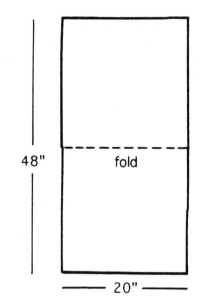

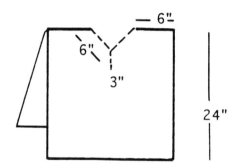

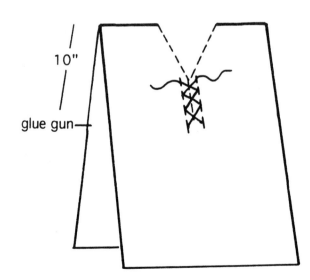

Fig. 1.16. Woodsman's hat.

Materials:

⅜ yd. of green, brown, or blue craft felt
Feather (optional)
Scissors
Glue gun

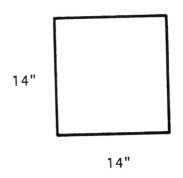

Construction:

- Cut a 14" x 14" square of felt.

- Fold the square in half.

- With the fold at the top, fold down corners and glue gun in place (see illustration).

- Add a feather if you wish.

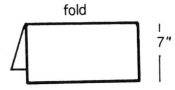

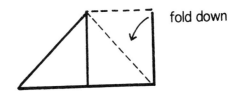

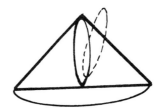

BIBLIOGRAPHY

Little Red Riding Hood *Versions*

Amery, H. *Little Red Riding Hood.* Tulsa, OK: Educational Development Corporation, 1987.

Coady, Christopher. *Red Riding Hood.* New York: Dutton Children's Books, 1992.

Crump, Fred. *Little Red Riding Hood.* Nashville, TN: Winston-Dereck, 1989.

de Regniers, Beatrice S. *Red Riding Hood.* New York: Aladdin Books, 1977.
    Retells in verse the adventures of a little girl who meets a wolf in the forest on her way to visit her grandmother.

Dyer, Jane. *Little Red Riding Hood.* New York: G. P. Putnam & Sons, 1985.

Edens, Cooper. *Little Red Riding Hood.* San Diego, CA: Green Tiger Press, 1989.
    Illustrated with pictures from different old books about Little Red Riding Hood.

Galdone, Paul. *Little Red Riding Hood.* New York: McGraw-Hill, 1974.

Hillert, Margaret. *Little Red Riding Hood.* Cleveland, OH: Modern Curriculum Press, 1981.

Hyman, Trina Schart. *Little Red Riding Hood.* Boston: Houghton Mifflin, 1989.

Mahans, Brenton. *Little Red Riding Hood.* Mawah, NJ: Troll Associates, 1981.

Marshall, James. *Little Red Riding Hood.* New York: Dial Books for Young Readers, 1987.

Montresor, Beni. *Little Red Riding Hood.* New York: Doubleday, 1991.

Schmidt, Karen. *Little Red Riding Hood.* New York: Scholastic, 1986.

Other Books

Bradman, Tony, and Margaret Chamberlain. *Look Out, He's Behind You!* New York: G. P. Putnam's Sons, 1988.
    Movable flaps conceal portions of the illustrations of this version of *Little Red Riding Hood.*

Brett, Jan. *The First Dog.* San Diego, CA: Harcourt Brace Jovanovich, 1988.
    The story of Paowolf, who becomes the first dog.

Carlson, Nancy. *A Visit to Grandma's.* New York: Viking Penguin, 1991.
    Tina visits her grandmother in her new Florida condominium and is surprised to find out how different she is from when she lived on the farm.

Cole, Babette. *The Trouble with Gran.* New York: G. P. Putnam's Sons, 1987.
    Gran, who is secretly an extraterrestrial being, livens up a trip to the seaside taken by a group of school children and senior citizens.

Delaney, A. *The Gunnywolf.* New York: Harper & Row, 1988.

A little girl wanders into the woods and meets the dreaded Gunnywolf. This story has its origins in an African-American folktale.

Dijs, Carla. *Little Red Riding Hood.* New York: Dell, 1991.

A pop-up book perfect for the youngest reader.

Emberly, Michael. *Ruby.* Boston, Toronto, London: Little, Brown & Co., 1990.

While taking cheese pies to her granny, Ruby, a street smart little mouse, forgets her mother's advice not to talk to cats.

Gackenbach, Dick. *With Love from Gran.* Boston: Houghton Mifflin, 1989.

A little boy's grandmother decides to see the world and sends him a present from each place she visits.

Gantschev, Grant. *The Train to Grandma's.* Saxonville, MA: Picture Book Studio, 1987.

Two children make a journey by train to visit their grandparents.

Goodall, John S. *Little Red Riding Hood.* New York: Margaret K. McElderry Books, 1988.

A wordless, half-page, lift-the-flap book about a little mouse.

Harper, Wilhelminia. *Gunniwolf.* New York: E. P. Dutton, 1946.

Little Girl wanders into the jungle to pick flowers and meets the Gunniwolf.

Hines, Anna Grossnickle. *Grandma Gets Grumpy.* New York: Clarion Books, 1988.

Five cousins visit their grandmother and discover there is a limit to her patience.

Kasza, Keiko. *The Wolf's Chicken Stew.* New York: G. P. Putnam's Sons., 1987.

A hungry wolf's attempts to fatten a chicken for his stew pot have unexpected results.

Ketner, Mary Grace. *Ganzy Remembers.* New York: Atheneum, 1991.

Ganzy tells stories about her childhood on a Texas farm.

Lemieux, Michele. *Peter and the Wolf.* New York: Morrow Junior Books, 1991.

Retells the orchestral fairy tale of the boy who, ignoring his grandfather's warnings, proceeds to capture a wolf.

Ross, Tony. *The Boy Who Cried Wolf.* New York: Dial Books for Young Readers, 1985.

A funny twist to an old fable, with an unexpected ending.

_____. *Stone Soup.* New York: Dial Books for Young Readers, 1987.

Mother Hen is going to be in the soup herself unless she can fend off the hungry big, bad wolf with her stone soup.

Ruis, Maria. *Grandparents.* New York: Barrons, 1987.

A simple explanation of what grandparents are and their place in the Anglo family. The book includes an information section about grandparents for teachers.

Seymour, Peter. *Little Red Riding Hood.* Los Angeles: Intervisual Communications, 1990.

A pop-up book with action characters.

Sharmat, Marjorie Weinman. *Walter the Wolf*. New York: Holiday House, 1975.

Tired of being perfect and never using his perfectly matched fangs, Walter the wolf yields to temptation.

Testa, Fulvio. *Wolf's Favor*. New York: Dial Books for Young Readers, 1986.

A cumulative tale about a wolf who does a favor for a porcupine, which leads to more favors done by a variety of animals.

Waddell, Martin. *Grandma's Bill*. New York: Orchard Books, 1990.

Little Bill learns about his grandfather Bill from his grandma's photograph album.

Wexco, John Bonnett. *ZOOBOOKS Wolves*. San Diego, CA: Wildlife Education Ltd., 1989.

Facts about wolves with photographs.

Williams, Barbara. *Kevin's Grandma*. New York: Dutton Children's Books, 1975.

Kevin's wacky grandma is not your typical grandmother. Instead of baking cookies and giving presents, for example, Kevin's grandmother rides a Honda 90, arm wrestles, and skydives.

Young, Ed. *Lon Po Po*. New York: Grosset & Dunlap, 1989.

A Red Riding Hood story from China.

Catalog

Safari, Ltd., Box 630685, Miami, FL 33163.

Carries authentic reproductions of animal and sea life. Write for a catalog.

Music

Copus, Pamela, and Joyce Harlow. "The Gunnywolf," *Story Play Music*. Englewood, CO: Teacher Ideas Press, 1992.

2

GOLDILOCKS AND THE THREE BEARS

DRAMA/PLAY EXPERIENCE

Introduce "Goldilocks and the Three Bears" by reading one of the many versions. (See bibliography, page 40, for this and other sources.) Janet Stevens's version remains true to the original story and is an excellent one to start with. After reading the story, demonstrate the simpletees costumes and the play props.

Simpletees Costumes

Use simpletees costumes of Goldilocks and the three bears for the dramatic play experience. (See figures 2.1 and 2.2.)

Play Props

The play props can include small, medium, and large bowls, spoons, cups, and chairs. Add a small table and three small quilts or blankets to serve as the beds. Include bear claw house slippers, which can be found at Christmastime in department stores or in mail-order catalogs.

Face Masks

Make face masks of Goldilocks and the three bears. Use tagboard templates to create the masks. (See figures 2.3 and 2.4.)

Stick Puppets/Paper Bag Theater

Make stick puppets of Goldilocks and the three bears. (See figure 2.5.) Create a paper bag theater for the stick puppets (see figure 1.7 on page 8). Present the play to a friend or take home and present to parents.

Fig. 2.1. Simpletees costumes: Goldilocks and the Three Bears.

Goldilocks

XL yellow,
short-sleeved
T-shirt

Glue gun 1 1/4 yd. lace ruffle
to bottom of T-shirt

Bears (make 3)

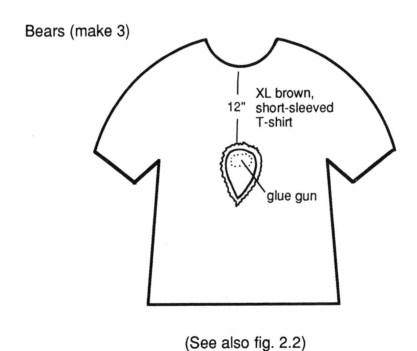

XL brown,
12"   short-sleeved
T-shirt

glue gun

(See also fig. 2.2)

Fig. 2.2. Bear tail pattern and directions.

Materials:

⅛ yd. brown fake fur
Scissors
Glue gun

What to Do:

Use pattern to cut 3 fur tails. (Cut on back side.)

Glue tail to center back of T-shirt 12" down from the neck.

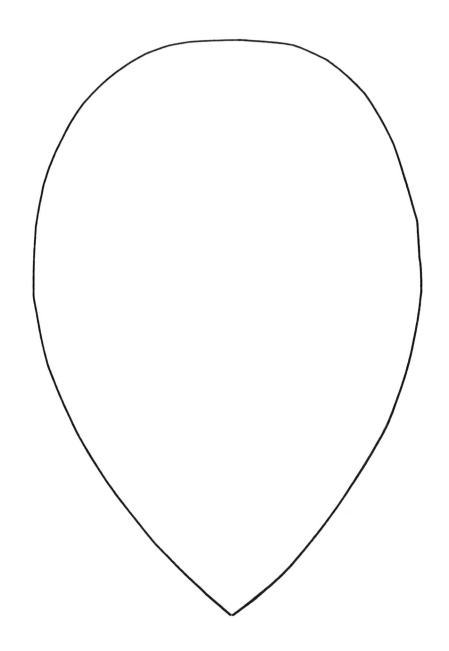

Fig. 2.3. Goldilocks face mask pattern.

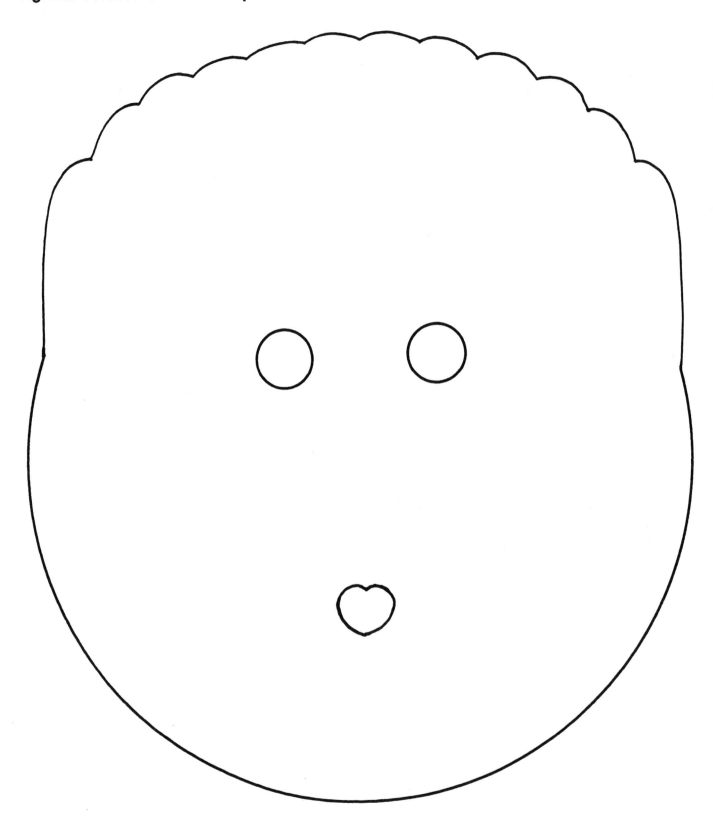

Fig. 2.4. Three Bears face mask pattern.

Fig. 2.5. Goldilocks and the Three Bears stick puppet patterns.

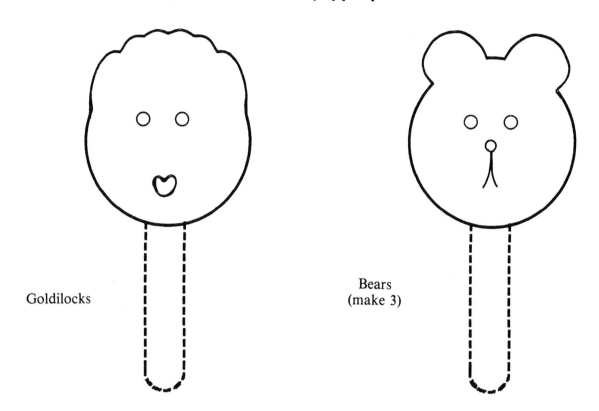

Goldilocks

Bears
(make 3)

LITERATURE/WRITING EXPERIENCE

Goldilocks and the Three Bears *Versions*

Read and discover how versions of "Goldilocks and the Three Bears" differ from each other. Paul Galdone's version is close to the original and an excellent way to introduce the story. In James Marshall's version, the three bears go for a ride on their bicycles while waiting for the porridge to cool. Jan Brett's illustrations provide a visual feast full of entrancing detail. Explore various versions and discuss how they are different.

Goldilocks and the Three Bears *Children's Version*

Write a children's version of "Goldilocks and the Three Bears" on a large sheet of chart paper. Plan a different ending or change the characters.

Key-Word Books and Key Words

Make a key-word book using the unique or important words in the story. The key words for "Goldilocks and the Three Bears" are as follows:

Goldilocks	three	bears
porridge	spoon	bowl
chair	bed	

Bear Shape Book

Make a bear shape book from tagboard templates. (See figure 2.6.) Staple the book together at the top. Illustrate the book and write the story or dictate it to the teacher. Use key words for an independent writing experience.

All About My Bear

Read *Teddy Bear Towers* by Bruce Degan. Bring a bear from home. Tell the class about your bear. Discuss where your bear came from. How old you were when you got your bear? Do you sleep with your bear? (Record the children's stories on a large sheet of chart paper.)

From *Story Play*, copyright 1992. Libraries Unlimited/Teacher Ideas Press, P.O. Box 6633, Englewood, CO 80155-6633.

Fig. 2.6. Bear shape book directions and pattern.

Materials:

Brown construction
  paper
Tagboard template
White paper
Markers or pencils
Scissors
Stapler
Key words

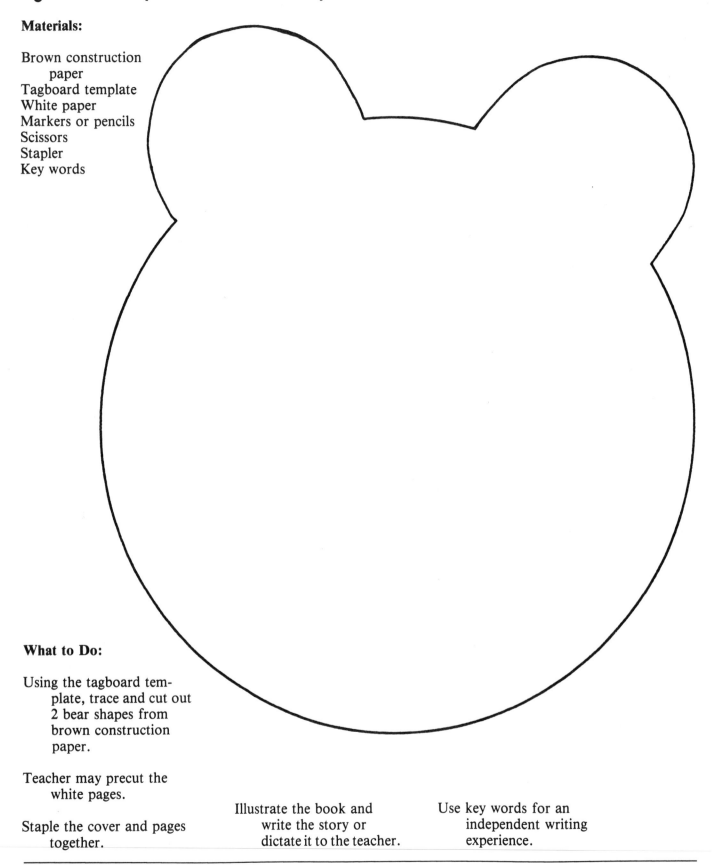

What to Do:

Using the tagboard tem-
  plate, trace and cut out
  2 bear shapes from
  brown construction
  paper.

Teacher may precut the
  white pages.

Staple the cover and pages
  together.

Illustrate the book and
  write the story or
  dictate it to the teacher.

Use key words for an
  independent writing
  experience.

COOPERATIVE/GROUP EXPERIENCE

Bear's Den

Plan and construct a bear's den from a large cardboard box. The box should be big enough to hold two children. Work in small groups and paint the box with brown tempera. Allow the paint to dry, then use black tempera or a marker to outline large boulders on the box. Add bear books to the den so you can share bear stories. Read *Could I Be?* by Joanne Oppenheim, a story about a hibernating bear. The teacher may decorate the den for added atmosphere.

Bear Feast

Participate in a bear feast before hibernating (nap time). Bring a small bag of one trail mix ingredient from home. Examples include peanuts, raisins, mini chocolate or butterscotch chips, shelled sunflower seeds, coconut, granola, and cereals. Empty all the ingredients into a large bowl and mix together with a small, a medium, and a large wooden spoon. Use a small scoop to measure the trail mix into small bags. Eat the trail mix in the bear's den.

Teddy Bear Picnic

Read *The Party* by David McPhail and *The Teddy Bears' Picnic* by Jimmy Kennedy. Bring a special bear from home. Celebrate the bear activities with a teddy bear picnic. The picnic may be held indoors or outside. Invite parents to participate.

Bird's-Eye View

Create a bird's-eye view picture like the ones on pages 23 and 24 of *The Teddy Bears' Picnic* by Jimmy Kennedy. How do you think something would look from the air? Place a piece of paper on the floor and look down at it. For instance, a tree may look like a big green circle. Demonstrate by drawing the circle. Work in small groups to add to the picture.

ART/WRITING EXPERIENCE

Tempera Paintings

Paint a picture of Goldilocks and the three bears. Use brown, yellow, and people colors. (People Colors™ crayons or tempera may be purchased at school supply stores.) People colors can also be obtained by adding a small amount of orange or different amounts of brown tempera to white tempera. Write a caption for the painting. Display the paintings on the walls or the bulletin board. Bind the paintings together to make a classroom book.

Bear Trail

Read *Animal Tracks* by Arthur Dorros, *Crinkleroot's Book of Animal Tracking* by Jim Arnosky, and *Making Tracks* by Stephen Savage. Use a bear paw stamp to make a bear trail across a long strip of paper or make a sponge paw print. Write or dictate the answer to the question "If a bear came to my house I would _____!" Animal paw print stamps may be purchased from teacher supply stores, card shops, or mail-order catalogs.

Goldilocks

Read *Ruby* by Maggie Glen. Ruby was different from the other bears; not everyone has yellow hair like Goldilocks. Cut different colors of construction paper into 1-inch strips. Roll the strips of paper around a pencil to make curly locks. Glue the locks around the top half of a small paper plate. Use markers to draw a face on the plate. Change the color of the locks to blue or green. Display the finished works on the walls or the bulletin board.

COOKING/MATH EXPERIENCE

Three Bears Porridge

Make Three Bears Porridge. Combine 3 tablespoon instant grits with 1 cup boiling water. Stir in 1 tablespoon powdered milk. Add 1 teaspoon honey. Take a Bear Walk while waiting for the porridge to cool. Taste the porridge and compare it to oatmeal and cream of wheat. Record which one you like the best on a graph.

Honey Bears

Make a honey bear by cutting a bear shape from a slice of whole wheat bread with a bear cookie cutter. Spread honey on the bear from a squeeze bottle and eat. Use the rebus recipe for an independent experience. (See figure 2.7.)

Bear Claw Cookies

Ice a sugar cookie with chocolate icing. Add five chocolate chips for paw pads. Use the rebus recipe for an independent experience. (See figure 2.8.)

Fig. 2.7. Honey bear.

1 slice

1 cutter

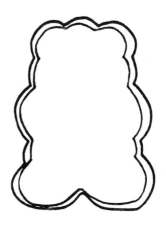

1 squeeze of honey

Three
Bears
Honey

Fig. 2.8. Bear claw cookie.

1 sugar cookie

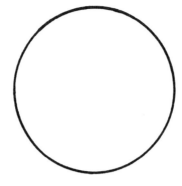

spread 1
teaspoon icing

add 5
chocolate chips

SCIENCE/DISCOVERY EXPERIENCE

Bear Facts

Learn facts about real bears. For example, bears hibernate in the winter. They prepare for winter by eating so much food that they get fat. They usually live alone. Bears seem friendly and playful, but they can be dangerous. Bears are meat-eating animals. They also eat acorns, berries, fruits, nuts, and the leaves and roots of plants. Bears are also fond of honey. A male bear is called a *boar* or *he-bear*. A female bear is called a *sow* or *she-bear*. A young bear is called a *cub*. (Add plastic models of real bears to the block center to extend the experience.)

Honeycomb

Examine a real honeycomb. (Sometimes honey bought from a local beekeeper is canned with the honeycomb in the jar.) Invite a beekeeper to your class. Eat honey from a small nut cup for a tasting experience.

MUSIC/POETRY/GAME EXPERIENCE

Teddy Bear Parade

Bring bears from home and carry them in a parade. Visit another class with the parade or take the bear parade outdoors.

Listen to any marching music or "The Bears Parade," performed by Pamela Copus. (See bibliography, page 41.) Move in synchronization with the music and pretend to be bears.

Fuzzy Wuzzy Choral Reading

Have a choral reading of "Fuzzy Wuzzy." Write the poem on a large sheet of chart paper. Repeat the poem after the teacher.

Fuzzy Wuzzy was a bear,

Fuzzy Wuzzy had no hair.

Fuzzy Wuzzy wasn't fuzzy.

Was he?

Clapping Rhyme: Pease Porridge Hot

Recite the Mother Goose rhyme "Pease Porridge Hot" while performing a clapping sequence. Hold two hands up and clap your partner's hands. Clap your own hands and then slap your thighs. Repeat your own hand clap and then clap your partner's hands again. Chant the rhyme to the rhythm of the hand claps.

Pease porridge hot, pease porridge cold,

Pease porridge in the pot, nine days old.

Some like it hot, some like it cold,

Some like it in the pot, nine days old.

Bear in the Pit

Form a circle while holding hands. Choose a bear to be in the center of the ring. The bear in the center tries to crawl out between two children, who then drop their hands and chase the bear. The one that tags the bear gets to be the next bear, and the game continues.

Bear Obstacle Course/Follow the Bear

Plan and construct a bear obstacle course either indoors or outside. Trace and cut out bear paw prints. (See figure 2.9.) Construct a path through the obstacle course or leading up to it. Play Follow the Bear and go through the course imitating the leader.

Fig. 2.9. Bear paw print pattern.

Materials:	What to Do:
Brown construction paper Tagboard template Markers or crayons Scissors	Use tagboard template to trace bear paw prints on brown construction paper. Cut out paw prints. Draw foot pads with markers or crayons.

SUPPLEMENTARY COSTUME PIECES

Instructions for making bear ears are in figure 2.10.

Fig. 2.10. Bear ears.

Materials:

⅛ yd. brown craft felt
12" strip of Velcro Sticky
    Back tape, ¾" wide
Scissors
Pins
Glue gun

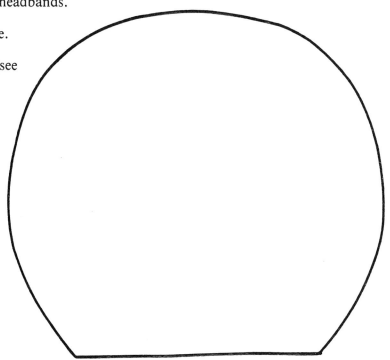

Velcro   (4"w x 24"l)

Construction:

- Use pattern to cut 6 brown felt bear ears.

- Cut 3 4" x 24" strips of brown felt for headbands.

- Fold headbands in half and pin in place.

- Glue gun 2 ears inside each headband (see illustration).

- Glue gun headbands together.

- Cut Velcro into 3 4" strips.

- Glue gun Velcro strips to ends of headbands.

BIBLIOGRAPHY

Goldilocks and the Three Bears *Versions*

Barton, Byron. *The Three Bears.* New York: HarperCollins, 1991.

Brett, Jan. *Goldilocks and the Three Bears.* New York: Dodd, Mead & Company, 1987.

Cauley, Lorinda. *Goldilocks and the Three Bears.* New York: G. P. Putnam's Sons, 1981.

Cosgrove, Stephen. *Goldilocks.* Nashville, TN: Ideals, 1988.

Dyer, Jane. *Goldilocks and the Three Bears.* New York: G. P. Putnam's Sons, 1984.

Eden, Cooper. *Goldilocks and the Three Bears.* San Diego, CA: Green Tiger Press, 1989.

Eisen, Armond. *Goldilocks and the Three Bears.* New York: Alfred A. Knopf, 1989.

Ferris, Lynn B. *Goldilocks and the Three Bears.* New York: Alfred A. Knopf, 1987.

Galdone, Paul. *Goldilocks and the Three Bears.* New York: Clarion Books, 1972.

Mahan, Benton. *Goldilocks and the Three Bears.* Mahwah, NJ: Troll Associates, 1981.

Marshall, James. *Goldilocks and the Three Bears.* New York: Dial Books for Young Readers, 1988.

Scally, Kevin. *The Three Bears.* New York: G. P. Putnam's Sons, 1984.

Stevens, Janet. *Goldilocks and the Three Bears.* New York: Holiday House, 1986.

Watts, Bernadette. *Goldilocks and the Three Bears.* Gossau Zürich, Switzerland: North-South Books, 1984.

Other Books

Arnosky, Jim. *Crinkleroot's Book of Animal Tracking.* New York: Bradbury Press, 1989.
  Explains how to find and understand the signs made by animals.

Brett, Jan. *Berlioz the Bear.* New York: G. P. Putnam's Sons, 1991.
  An orchestra of bears is due to play for the town ball when their bandwagon becomes stuck.

Bullaty, Sonja, and Angelo Lomeo. *The Baby Bears.* New York: Western, 1983.
  Contains photographs of real bears taken in the Great Smoky Mountains.

Cole, Joanna. *Anna Banana.* New York: Morrow Junior Books, 1989.
  A collection of jump rope rhymes including "Teddy Bear, Teddy Bear."

Degan, Bruce. *Teddy Bear Towers.* New York: HarperCollins, 1991.
  A land of teddy bears is ruled by a little boy who will not let his younger brother play.

Dorros, Arthur. *Animal Tracks.* New York: Scholastic, 1991.
    Introduces the tracks and signs left by animals.

Glen, Maggie. *Ruby.* New York: G. P. Putnam's Sons, 1990.
    Ruby, a teddy bear, is accidently made out of the wrong material and gets the letter "S" stamped on her paw. She thinks the "S" means "special" until someone tells her it means "seconds."

Johnston, Tony. *Little Bear Sleeping.* New York: G. P. Putnam's Sons, 1991.
    A sleepy bear tries to convince his mother that it isn't time for bed. The story is told in verse.

Kennedy, Jimmy. *The Teddy Bears' Picnic.* San Diego, CA: Green Tiger Press, 1983.
    Every bear that ever was gathers in the woods for a picnic.

McPhail, David. *The Party.* Boston: Joy Street Books, 1990.

Oppenheim, Joanne. *Could I Be?* New York: Dell, 1990.
    Surrounded by the many sounds of spring, a hibernating bear is late waking up until he hears one very special sound.

Savage, Stephen. *Making Tracks.* Los Angeles: Intervisual Communications, 1992.
    A pull of the slide on each page of this unique book reveals first a track and then the identity of the animal who made it.

Schoenherr, John. *Bear.* New York: Philomel Books, 1991.
    A realistic book about a little bear who loses his mother and learns to fend for himself.

Tolhurst, Marilyn. *Somebody and the Three Blairs.* New York: Orchard Books, 1990.
    A reversal of Goldilocks, in which a bear visits the home of the Blairs.

Tomkins, Jasper. *When a Bear Bakes a Cake.* San Diego, CA: Green Tiger Press, 1987.
    A story told in verse about a bear who bakes a cake and throws it in the lake.

Turkel, Brinton. *Deep in the Forest.* New York: Dutton Children's Books, 1976.
    A wordless picture book about a little bear who visits a family in a reversal of the traditional tale.

Music

Copus, Pamela, and Joyce Harlow. "The Bears' Parade." *Story Play Music.* Englewood, CO: Teacher Ideas Press, 1992.

THE THREE LITTLE PIGS

DRAMA/PLAY EXPERIENCE

Set the stage for the dramatic play experience by introducing the theme with a story of "The Three Little Pigs." An excellent one to start with is James Marshall's version, which remains close to the original. (See bibliography, page 56, for this and other sources.) After reading the story, introduce and demonstrate the costumes and play props.

Simpletees Costumes

Use simpletees costumes of the three little pigs, the mama pig, and the wolf for the dramatic play experience. (See figures 3.1 and 3.2.)

Play Props

The play props can include pig food: plastic apples, carrots, corn, or any raw vegetable will do. Put the vegetables in wicker baskets for added atmosphere. Add a small table, chairs, dishes, and a large cloth napkin for the table cover. Include a purse, hat, and apron for the mama pig.

Face Masks

Create face masks of the mama pig, the three little pigs, and the wolf. (See figures 3.3 and 3.4, in addition to figure 1.4 on page 5.)

Stick Puppets/Paper Bag Theater

Make stick puppets of the mama pig, the three little pigs and the wolf. (See figure 3.5.) Create a paper bag theater for the stick puppets. (See figure 1.7 on page 8.) Present the play to a friend or take home and present to parents.

Woodworking Experience

Experience "woodworking" with the little pig who made his house of wood. Use roofing nails, a tool box, a hammer, and safety goggles. Hammer the nails into a stump or a log. You can do the woodworking either indoors or outside.

Fig. 3.1. Simpletees costumes: The Three Little Pigs.

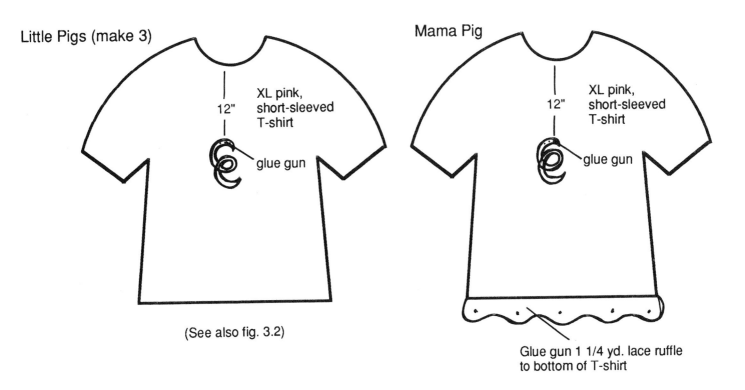

Little Pigs (make 3)

12"

XL pink,
short-sleeved
T-shirt

glue gun

(See also fig. 3.2)

Mama Pig

12"

XL pink,
short-sleeved
T-shirt

glue gun

Glue gun 1 1/4 yd. lace ruffle
to bottom of T-shirt

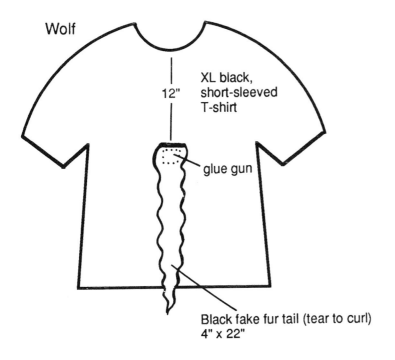

Wolf

12"

XL black,
short-sleeved
T-shirt

glue gun

Black fake fur tail (tear to curl)
4" x 22"

Fig. 3.2. Pig tail pattern and directions.

Materials:

⅛ yd. of pink craft felt
Scissors
Glue gun

What to Do:

Use pattern to cut 8 pink felt pig tails.

Double tails and glue together (this makes the tails stronger).

Glue top of tail 12" down from the neck of the T-shirt.

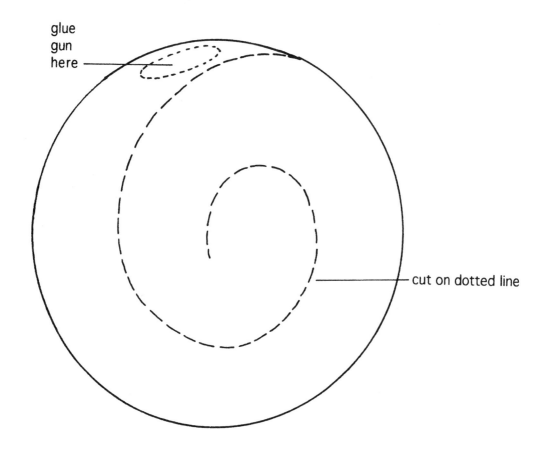

glue
gun
here

cut on dotted line

Fig. 3.3. Mama pig face mask pattern.

Fig. 3.4. Little pigs face mask pattern.

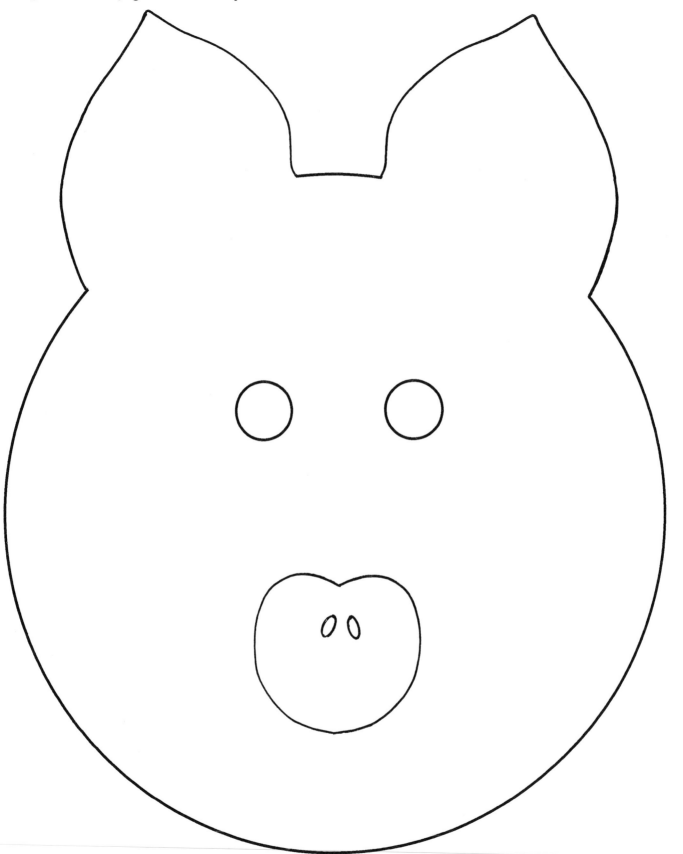

Fig. 3.5. Three Little Pigs stick puppet patterns.

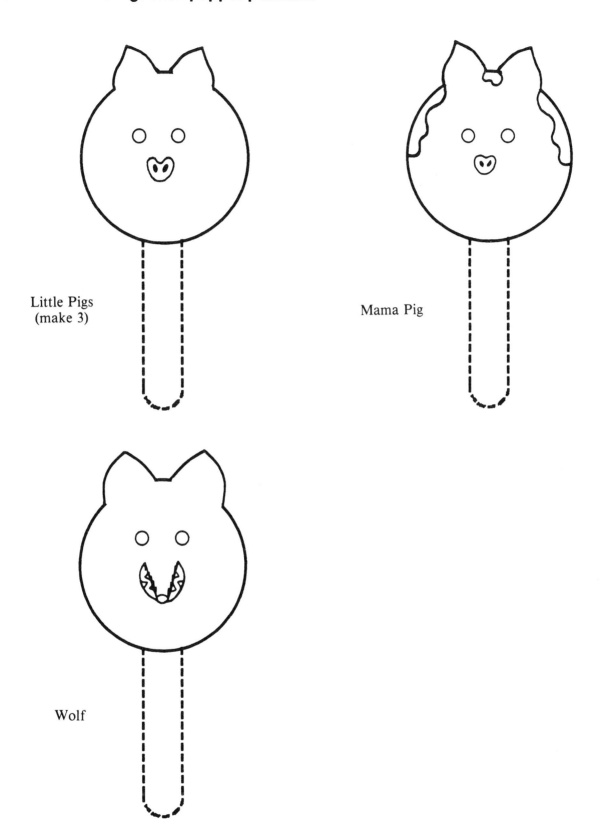

Little Pigs
(make 3)

Mama Pig

Wolf

LITERATURE/WRITING EXPERIENCE

The Three Little Pigs *Versions*

Read and discover how versions of "The Three Little Pigs" differ from each other. (See bibliography on page 56.) For example, in *The Three Little Pigs and the Fox* by William Hooks, the smartest little pig is a girl and the villain is a fox. Gavin Bishop's version remains close to the original, while Jon Scieszka tells the story from the wolf's point of view. Explore various versions and discuss how they are different.

The Three Little Pigs *Children's Version*

After reading the different versions of "The Three Little Pigs," write a children's version. The villain could be a gorilla or a dragon. Discuss how the version will end.

Key-Word Books and Key Words

Make a key-word book using the unique or important words in the story. The key words for "The Three Little Pigs" are as follows:

three	little	pigs
wolf	house	turnip
apple	straw	stick
brick		

Little Pig Shape Book

Make a little pig shape book. (See figure 3.6.) Trace and cut out two pig shapes for the outside covers of the book. Illustrate the book and write the story or dictate it to the teacher. Use key words for an independent writing experience.

Fig. 3.6. Little pigs shape book directions and pattern.

Materials:

Pink construction paper
Tagboard template
White paper
Scissors
Stapler
Markers or crayons
Key words

What to Do:

Using the tagboard
template, trace and cut
out 2 pig shapes from
pink construction paper.

Teacher may precut
white pages.

Staple the cover and
pages together.

Illustrate the book
and write the story
or dictate it to the
teacher.

Use the key words
for an independent
writing experience.

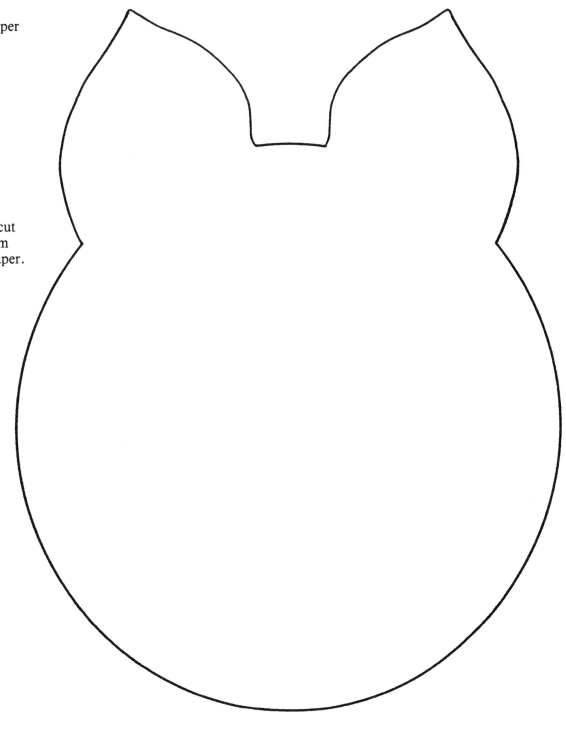

COOPERATIVE/GROUP EXPERIENCE

Mud Pie Factory

Read *The Piggy in the Puddle* by Charlotte Pomerantz and *Muddy Millford* by Mark Southgate. Set up a mud pie factory and make real mud pies. Dig the dirt or use top soil from a nursery or garden supply store. Use a wooden spoon to mix the soil with water. Form the mud into small balls and flatten the balls with your hands. Sell mud pies to a friend. Use leaves or grass for money if your factory is outside. Brown playdough can be substituted for the mud.

Three Pigs Houses

Make a straw, a stick, and a brick house from large cardboard boxes. Use wardrobe boxes from a moving company. Paint and decorate the houses. Use yellow paint for the straw house, brown paint for the stick house, and red paint for the brick house.

Use simpletees costumes with the houses and present a play for another class or for parents.

Brick Factory

Establish a brick factory. Set up an assembly line and stuff paper bags with crumpled or shredded paper. Staple or tape the bag tops together to form "bricks." Use the bricks plain or paint them red. Use the finished bricks to build the third little pig's house. You can set up the brick factory either indoors or outside.

Straw House

Purchase a bale of hay or straw and place it on the playground. Use the straw or hay to construct the first little pig's house. Add a large cardboard box to provide another dimension to the problem of building a straw house. An opening in the box can serve as the door to a room inside the box. The box should be large enough for a child to sit in.

ART/WRITING EXPERIENCE

Tempera Paintings

Paint a picture of the three little pigs. Use pink, yellow, brown, and red tempera. Write a caption for the painting. Display the paintings on the walls or the bulletin board. Bind the paintings together to make a book.

Miniature Pig Houses

Make a miniature pig house. Paint a small milk carton yellow, brown, or red. Glue moving doll's eyes purchased from a craft store on a pink cotton ball and place the "pig" inside the house. (Precut a door on one side of the carton.)

Thumbprint Pigs

Make thumbprint pigs. Use a red ink pad to make thumbprints and add tails and eyes with a black marker. Make a cartoon strip of pigs. Use black ink to make a thumbprint wolf. Add a tail and ears to the wolf with a black marker. Make word balloons and write a dialogue on the cartoon. Word balloons can be made from self-sticking labels.

COOKING/MATH EXPERIENCE

Huff 'n Puff Cake

Bake a Huff 'n Puff cake. Using a prepared mix, make an angel food cake according to the package directions. Eat the cake while it is still warm.

Pig Food

Read *Pig in a Barrow* by Bert Kitchen. Sample pig food. Examine and taste raw turnips and apples. Sort the apples by color and variety. After conducting a taste test, draw your favorite pig food on a small piece of paper and place the drawings on a simple bar graph. Compare the results of the graph.

Banana Pig Pudding

Make banana pig pudding. Crumble a fig bar in a small paper cup. Add banana slices. Top with whipped cream.

Pig Face Cookies

Make pig face cookies. Use a rebus recipe chart for an independent experience. (See figure 3.7.) Ice sugar cookies with pink icing. Use red hots for the eyes and pieces of cereal for the nose and ears.

Trifold Book

Make a trifold book. (See figure 3.8.) Sponge-stamp three pigs on one side and three houses on the other side. Show the one-to-one correspondence on the trifold book.

Fig. 3.7. Pig face cookies.

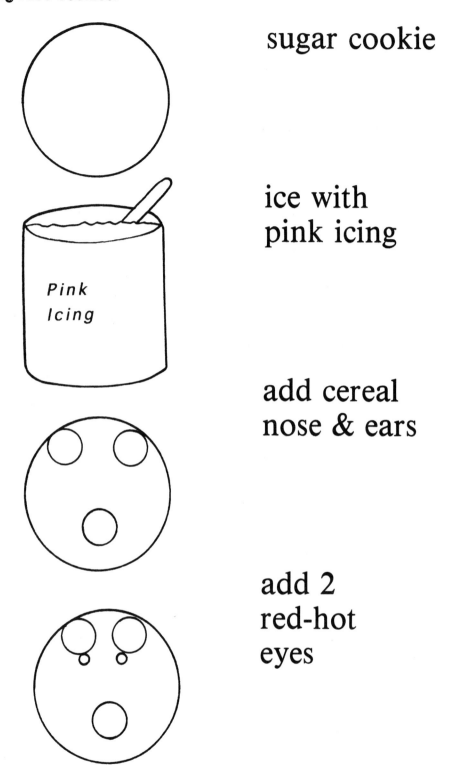

sugar cookie

ice with
pink icing

*Pink
Icing*

add cereal
nose & ears

add 2
red-hot
eyes

Fig. 3.8. Three Little Pigs trifold book directions and pattern.

Materials:

Paper strip (5" x 18")
Sponge pig stamp
Sponge house stamp
Pink tempera
Yellow, brown, red tempera

What to Do:

Fold paper in thirds accordion style.

Sponge-paint pink pigs in the three spaces on one side of paper.

Sponge-paint yellow, brown, and red houses on the other side of the paper.

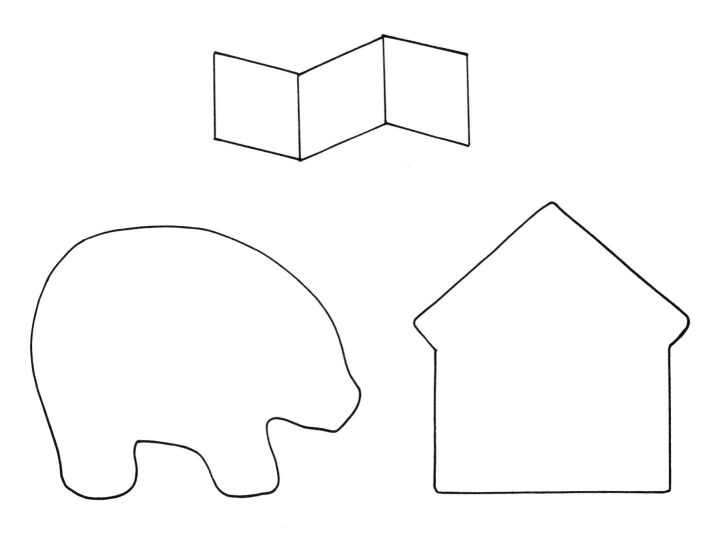

SCIENCE/DISCOVERY EXPERIENCE

Pig Facts

A *boar* is an adult male hog. A *sow* is an adult female hog. A *pig* is a hog that is less than 10 weeks old. A group of pigs is a *litter*. Hogs like to wallow in mud because it helps protect them from insects and keeps them cool. A hog's nose is called a *snout*. The snout is used to root or dig for vegetable roots. Hogs have short tails that are usually curly. They squeal or grunt when hurt or excited.

Vegetable Market

Read *Growing Vegetable Soup* by Lois Ehlert. The word *vegetable* refers to the stem, leaves, roots, and fruits of plants. Bring one vegetable from home for the market. Display and label the vegetables by name. Sort the vegetables by their color, for example red, yellow, or green. Wash, peel, and eat the raw vegetables for a tasting experience or cook them for vegetable soup.

MUSIC/POETRY/GAME EXPERIENCE

Pig Music

Sing "Piggy" to the tune of "Bingo."

> There was a farmer had a pig,
>
> and Piggy was his name-o.
>
> P-I-G-G-Y, P-I-G-G-Y, P-I-G-G-Y,
>
> And Piggy was his name-o!

Pig Choral Readings

Perform a choral reading from the story of "The Three Little Pigs." Read the following lines out loud at the appropriate places in the story.

> Little pig, little pig, let me come in.
>
> No, no, not by the hair of my chinny chin chin.
>
> Then I'll huff and I'll puff and I'll blow your house in.

Write the poem "I Had a Little Pig" on chart paper. Use the poem for a choral reading.

> I had a little pig,
>
> I fed him in a trough,
>
> He got so fat
>
> His tail dropped off.
>
> So I got me a hammer,
>
> And I got me a nail,
>
> And I made my little pig
>
> A brand-new tail.

If available, listen to the music "I Had a Little Pig" performed by Randy Copus. (See bibliography, page 57.) Chant the poem to the beat of the music. Use hand and thigh claps for accompaniment.

Steal the Bacon Game

Divide the class in half and have one team be the Pigs and the other team be the Wolves. Team members number off: one, two, three, and so one. The teams face each other about 10 feet apart. Put pretend bacon in the middle of the space between the teams. When you call out a number, the two opposing players with that number try to steal the bacon and run back to their side without being tagged. A player who is tagged becomes a member of the other team. The team with the most players at the end wins.

Big Bad Wolf Game

This game is similar to "Policeman, Policeman, My Child Is Lost." Three children are chosen to be the three little pigs. The pigs sit in chairs with their backs to the class. A wolf is chosen and hides in the room or outside the door. The wolf calls out in a disguised voice, "Little pigs, little pigs, let me come in." Each pig has one guess to identify the wolf. The game continues with new pigs and wolf.

SUPPLEMENTARY COSTUME PIECES

Instructions for making pig ears are in figure 3.9.

Fig. 3.9. Pig ears.

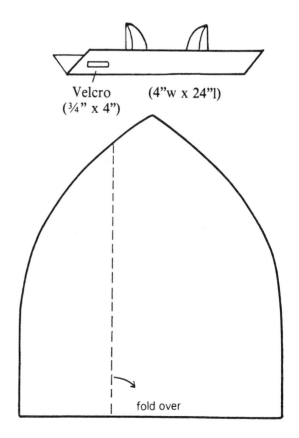

Materials:

1/8 yd. of pink craft felt
16" strip of Velcro Sticky Back tape, ¾" wide
Scissors
Pins
Glue gun

Construction:

- Use pattern to cut 8 pink felt pig ears
  (cut 16 and double ears to make them stronger).

- Cut 4 4" x 24" strips of pink felt for headbands.

- Fold headbands in half and pin in place.

- Glue gun ears inside headbands.

- Glue gun headband together.

- Cut Velcro into 4 4" strips.

- Glue gun Velcro strips to ends of headbands.

BIBLIOGRAPHY

The Three Little Pigs *Versions*

Blegvad, Eric. *The Three Little Pigs.* New York: Atheneum, 1980.

Bishop, Gavin. *The Three Little Pigs.* New York: Scholastic, 1989.

Claverie, Jean. *The Three Little Pigs.* Gossau Zurich, Switzerland: North-South Books, 1989.

Galdone, Paul. *The Three Little Pigs.* New York: Clarion Books, 1970.

Greenway, Jennifer. *The Three Little Pigs.* Kansas City, MO: Ariel Books, 1991.

Hayes, Sarah. *The Three Little Pigs.* New York: Crown, 1986.

Jose, Eduard. *The Three Little Pigs: A Classic Tale.* Elgin, IL: Child's World, 1989.

Leonard, Marcia. *The Three Little Pigs.* Englewood Cliffs, NJ: Silver Press, 1990.

Marshall, James. *The Three Little Pigs.* New York: Dial Books for Young Readers, 1989.

McGill-Franzen, Anne. *The Three Little Pigs.* New York: Crown, 1986.

Ross, Tony. *The Three Little Pigs.* New York: Pantheon, 1983.

Zemach, Margot. *The Three Little Pigs.* New York: Sunburst Books, 1988.

Other Books

Dunrea, Olivier. *Eddy B. Pigboy.* New York: Macmillan, 1983.
    Eddy's job is to make sure that the pigs do not wander off the farm.

Ehlert, Lois. *Growing Vegetable Soup.* San Diego, CA: Harcourt Brace Jovanovich, 1987.
    A father and child grow vegetables and then make them into soup.

Geisert, Arthur. *Oink.* Boston: Houghton Mifflin, 1991.
    When their mother falls asleep, the baby pigs sneak away, get into trouble, and must be rescued.

_____. *Pigs from A to Z.* Boston: Houghton Mifflin, 1986.
    Find the pigs that are hiding on each page.

Hellard, Susan. *This Little Piggy.* New York: G. P. Putnam's Sons, 1989.
    A lift-the-flap book about the traditional Mother Goose rhyme.

Hooks, William. *The Three Little Pigs and the Fox.* New York: Macmillan, 1989.
    An Appalachian version of the classic folktale, with an accent and twist all its own. The third little pig is a girl and the villain is a fox.

Hopkins, Bennett. *On the Farm.* Boston: Little, Brown & Company, 1991.
 A collection of poems about farms and farm animals.

Kitchen, Bert. *Pig in a Barrow.* New York: Dial Books for Young Readers, 1991.

Lobel, Arnold. *The Book of Pigericks.* New York: Harper & Row, 1983.
 A book of 38 original limericks about all manner of pigs.

_____. *A Treeful of Pigs.* New York: Scholastic, 1979.
 A lazy farmer promises to help his wife when pigs grow in trees like apples.

Most, Bernard. *The Cow That Went Oink.* San Diego, CA: Harcourt Brace Jovanovich, 1990.
 A cow that oinks and a pig that moos are ridiculed by the other barnyard animals until each teaches the other a new sound.

Pomerantz, Charlotte. *The Piggy in the Puddle.* New York: Macmillan, 1974.
 Unable to dissuade a young pig from playing in the mud, her family finally joins her for a mud party.

Scieszka, Jon. *The True Story of the Three Little Pigs by A. Wolf.* New York: Viking Penguin, 1989.
 The wolf gives his version of what really happened with the three little pigs.

Scott, Jack. *The Book of the Pig.* New York: G. P. Putnam's Sons, 1981.
 A nonfiction book about pigs.

Southgate, Mark. *Muddy Millford.* London: Blackie and Son, 1990.
 A lovely pink piglet needs a bath after discovering the joys of mud.

Varekamp, Marjolein. *Little Sam Takes a Bath.* New York: Orchard Books, 1991.
 A pull-the-tab peephole book about a little pig and his bath.

Wallner, John. *The Three Little Pigs.* New York: Viking Penguin, 1987.
 The story is told in rebus form with lift-up flaps and pop-up scenes.

Wood, Don, and Audrey Wood. *Piggies.* San Diego, CA: Harcourt Brace Jovanovich, 1991.
 Ten little piggies dance on a young child's fingers and toes before finally going to sleep.

Music

Copus, Pamela, and Joyce Harlow. "I Had a Little Pig." *Story Play Music.* Englewood, CO: Teacher Ideas Press, 1992.

THE LITTLE RED HEN

DRAMA/PLAY EXPERIENCE

Set the stage for the dramatic play experience by reading the story of "The Little Red Hen." (See bibliography, page 82, for this and other sources.) An excellent one to start with is Paul Galdone's version. His characters of the cat, the dog, and the mouse are featured as the simpletees costumes. After reading the story, demonstrate the costumes and play props for "The Little Red Hen."

Simpletees Costumes

Use simpletees costumes of the red hen, the cat, the dog, and the mouse for the dramatic play experience. (See figures 4.1, 4.2, and 4.3.)

Play Props

The play props can include a small table, a broom, and an apron. Add a plastic loaf of bread, plastic eggs, a wooden spoon, and a mixing bowl.

Face Masks

Create face masks of the red hen, the cat, the dog, and the mouse. Use tagboard templates to create the individual masks. (See figures 4.4, 4.5, 4.6, and 4.7.)

Stick Puppets/Paper Bag Theater

Make stick puppets of the red hen, the cat, the dog, and the mouse. (See figure 4.8.) Create a paper bag theater for the stick puppets. (See figure 1.7 on page 8.) Perform "The Little Red Hen" for a friend or take home and present to parents.

Fig. 4.1. Simpletees costumes: The Little Red Hen.

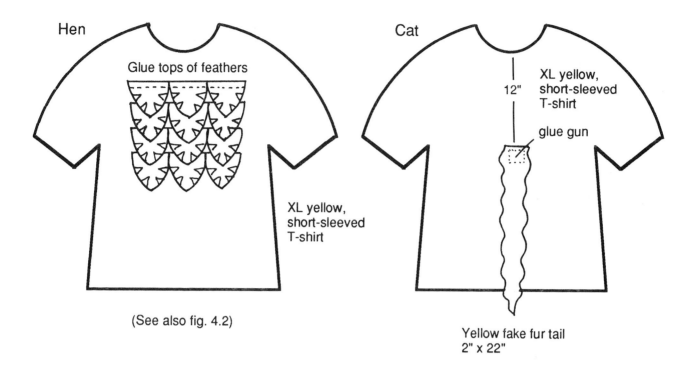

Hen

Glue tops of feathers

XL yellow,
short-sleeved
T-shirt

(See also fig. 4.2)

Cat

12"   XL yellow,
short-sleeved
T-shirt

glue gun

Yellow fake fur tail
2" x 22"

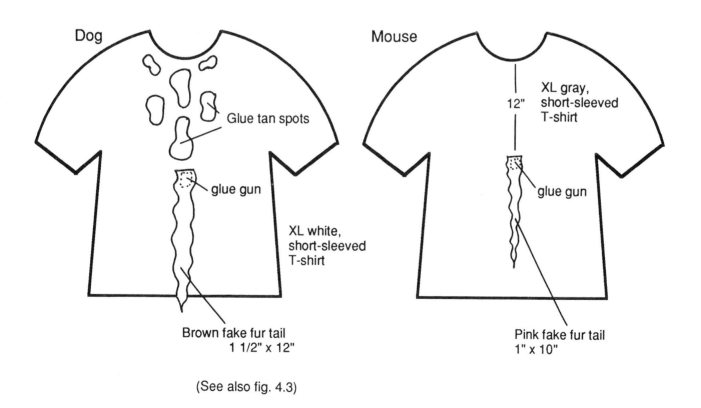

Dog

Glue tan spots

glue gun

XL white,
short-sleeved
T-shirt

Brown fake fur tail
1 1/2" x 12"

Mouse

12"   XL gray,
short-sleeved
T-shirt

glue gun

Pink fake fur tail
1" x 10"

(See also fig. 4.3)

Fig. 4.2. Hen feather directions and pattern.

Materials:

⅛ yd. of red craft felt
Scissors
Pins
Glue gun

Construction:

- Use pattern to cut 12 red felt feathers.

- Glue top edges of feathers to back of yellow
  T-shirt.

- Overlap feathers in rows of 3 each, making a total
  of 4 rows.

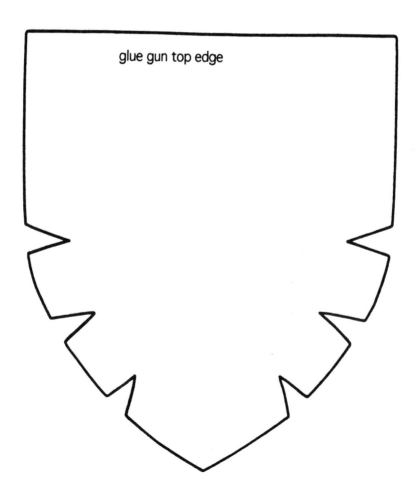

glue gun top edge

Fig. 4.3. Dog spot directions and patterns.

Materials:

⅛ yd. of tan felt
Scissors
Glue gun

Construction:

- Use patterns to cut 2 of each spot from tan felt.

- Glue spots to T-shirt.

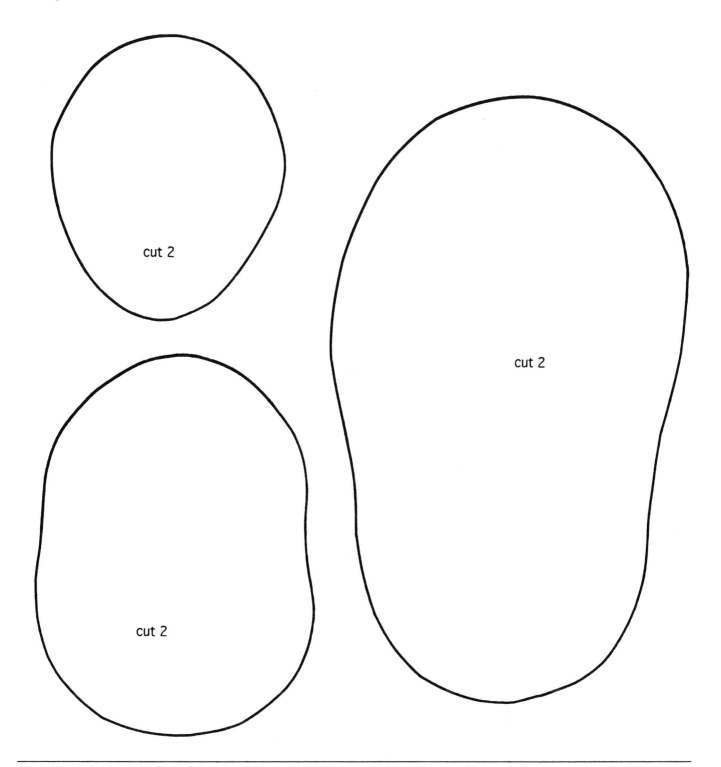

Fig. 4.4. Little Red Hen face mask pattern.

Fig. 4.5. Cat face mask pattern.

Fig. 4.6. Dog face mask pattern.

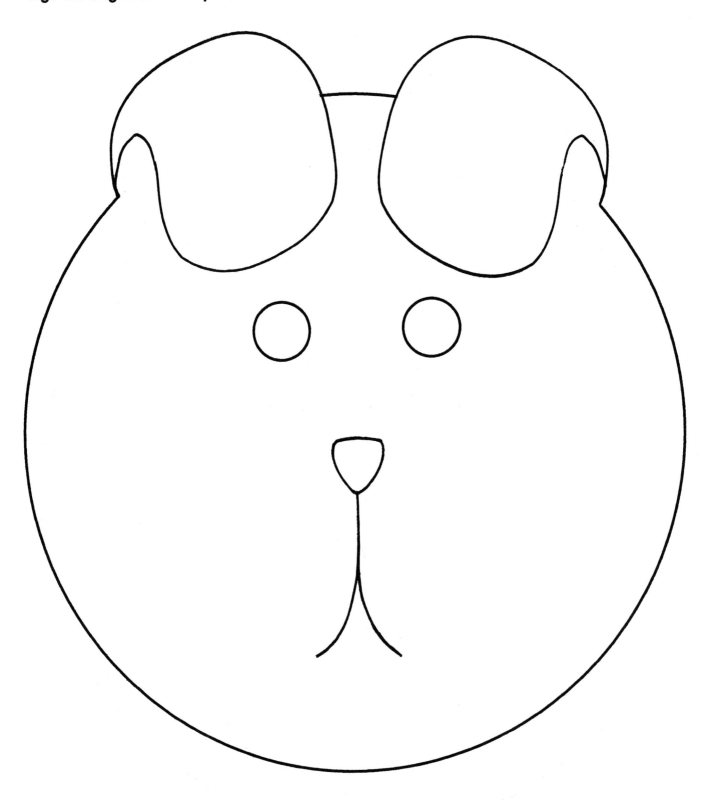

Fig. 4.7. Mouse face mask pattern.

Fig. 4.8. Little Red Hen stick puppet patterns.

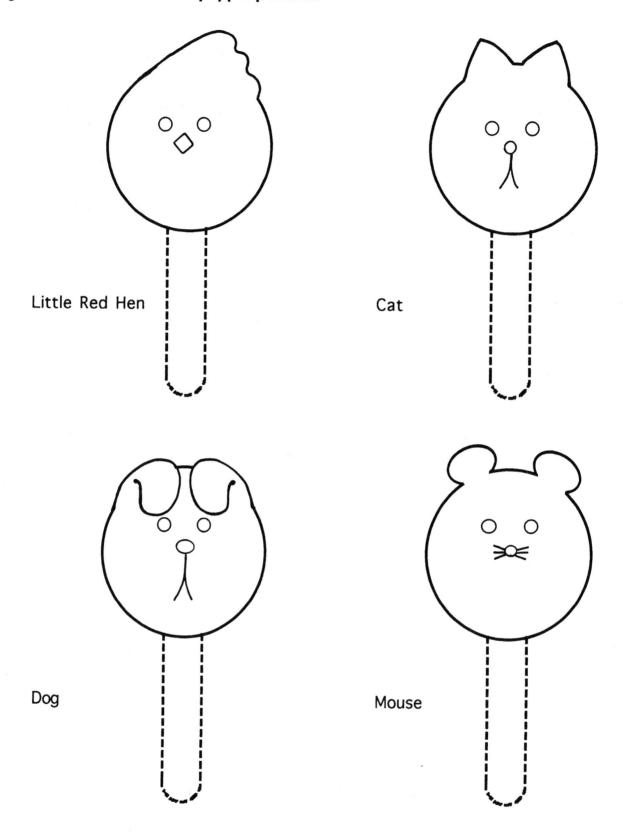

Little Red Hen

Cat

Dog

Mouse

LITERATURE/WRITING EXPERIENCE

The Little Red Hen *Versions*

Read and discover how versions of "The Little Red Hen" differ from each other. For example, in Lucinda McQueen's *The Little Red Hen* the main characters are a hen, a goose, a cat, and a dog. In Paul Galdone's version the main characters are a hen, a cat, a dog, and a mouse. Explore various versions and discuss the differences among them.

The Little Red Hen *Children's Version*

Write a children's version of "The Little Red Hen." Decide upon the characters, plot, and ending of the story.

Key-Word Books and Key Words

Make a key-word book with the unique or important words in the story. The key words for "The Little Red Hen" are as follows:

little	red	hen
cat	dog	mouse
wheat	mill	bread
flour		

Quill Pen Writing

Make a quill pen. Cut a slant at the tip of a chicken or turkey feather's quill. Dip the end of the quill in ink or tempera and write with it.

Little Red Hen Shape Book

Make a little red hen shape book by tracing the hen shape from a tagboard template. (See figure 4.9.) Illustrate the book and write the story or dictate it to the teacher. Use key words for an independent writing experience.

Fig. 4.9. Little Red Hen shape book directions and pattern.

Materials:

Red construction paper
Tagboard template
White paper
Markers or pencils
Scissors
Stapler
Key words

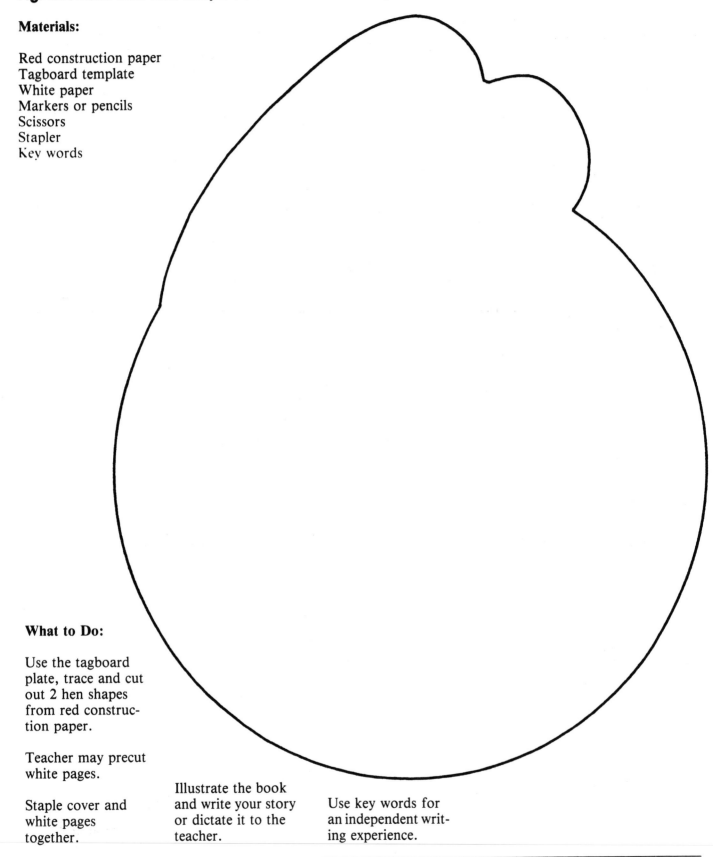

What to Do:

Use the tagboard
plate, trace and cut
out 2 hen shapes
from red construc-
tion paper.

Teacher may precut
white pages.

Staple cover and
white pages
together.

Illustrate the book
and write your story
or dictate it to the
teacher.

Use key words for
an independent writ-
ing experience.

From *Story Play*, copyright 1992. Libraries Unlimited/Teacher Ideas Press, P.O. Box 6633, Englewood, CO 80155-6633.

COOPERATIVE/GROUP EXPERIENCE

Little Red Hen Cottage

Design the little red hen's cottage from a large wardrobe box. Open the box at the seam and turn inside out to make a blank surface to paint on. Paint the cottage with red tempera. Make construction paper tiles for the roof. Use simpletees costumes of the red hen, the cat, the dog, and the mouse with the cottage and present a play for another class or for parents.

Chicken Walk

Read and discuss *Rosie's Walk* by Pat Hutchins and *I Went Walking* by Sue Williams. Plan a chicken walk. Make a chicken vest from a large paper grocery bag. Cut feathers from tagboard templates and glue them to the vest. (See figures 4.10 and 4.11.) Make chicken feet to go with your vest. (See figure 4.12.) Wear the vest and feet to go on a chicken walk either indoors or outside.

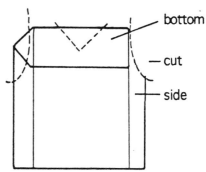

Fig. 4.10. Chicken vest pattern.

Materials:

Large grocery bag
Scissors

Construction:

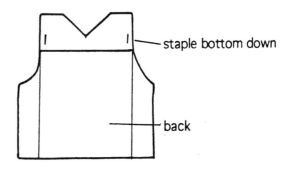

- Push out sides of bag to flatten.

- Staple bottom of bag to make vest flat instead of boxy.

- Cut out armholes.

- Cut V-neck opening.

- Cut center front open.

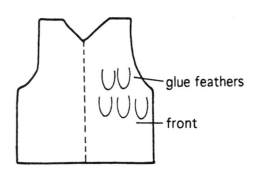

Fig. 4.11. Chicken feather directions and pattern.

Materials:

Red construction paper
Tagboard template
Markers or pencils
Scissors
Glue sticks

What to Do:

Using tagboard template, trace and cut out feather shapes from red construction paper.

Glue feathers to front and back of vest.

Fig. 4.12. Chicken feet directions and pattern.

Materials:

Yellow construction paper
Tagboard template
Markers or pencils
Scissors
Tape

What to Do:

Using tagboard template, trace and cut out two chicken feet from yellow construction paper.

Use tape to fasten the chicken feet around your ankles.

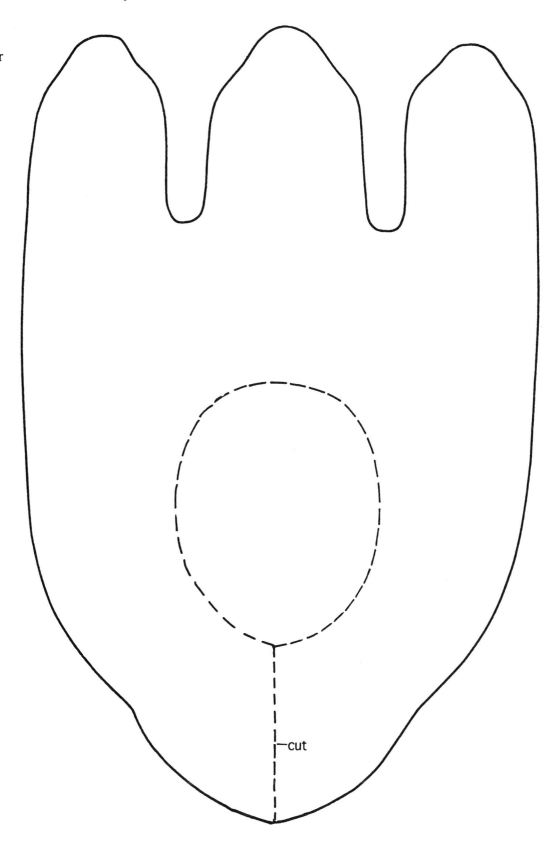

cut

From *Story Play*, copyright 1992. Libraries Unlimited/Teacher Ideas Press, P.O. Box 6633, Englewood, CO 80155-6633.

ART/WRITING EXPERIENCE

Tempera Paintings

Paint a picture of the Little Red Hen. Use red, yellow, and green tempera. Write a caption for the painting. Display the paintings on the walls or the bulletin board. Bind the paintings together to make a book.

Paint with a Feather

Choose a feather and gently move it to the rhythm of any selection of classical music. Switch the feather to your other hand and back again. Sit, stand up, and lie down as the music plays.

As you continue to listen to the music, paint with the feather. Dip the feather into thin tempera and gently brush it across the paper.

If available, "Paint with a Feather" performed by Pamela Copus may be used with this activity. (See bibliography, page 83.)

COOKING/MATH EXPERIENCE

Breadtasting

Read and discuss Ken Heyman's *Bread Bread Bread*, which features a visual feast of breads from around the world. Taste wheat, rye, pumpernickel, and white bread. Cut a bread-shaped piece of paper to represent your favorite bread. Use dark brown construction paper for rye, medium brown for wheat, black for pumpernickel, and white for white bread. Graph the favorite breads by placing the cut-out bread shapes on a bar graph. Compare the results.

Breadbaking

Place frozen loaves of wheat bread in loaf pans to thaw. Set the bread in a warm place and watch it rise. Inhale the yeast smell. Bake the bread, slice, and eat it while it is warm.

Henny Pennies

For a special treat, make Henny Pennies according to the following directions.

Mix in a blender: 1 5-ounce jar cheese spread

¼ cup shortening

⅔ cup all-purpose flour

Chill the dough 2 hours or overnight. Place one teaspoonful of dough on a floured surface and roll the Henny Penny with your hand until it is coated with flour. Place the Henny Pennies on an ungreased cookie sheet and flatten them with a fork. Bake at 375° for 12 to 15 minutes or until the Henny Pennies are slightly brown.

Measuring and Pouring Grain

Measure grain and pour it into a small tub or water playtable. Use measuring spoons, cups, and funnels. Popcorn is an excellent grain to use. Use a whisk broom and dustpan for independent cleanups.

SCIENCE/DISCOVERY EXPERIENCE

Egg Facts

Find out about eggs. Read *Chickens Aren't the Only Ones* by Ruth Heller, *Chick* by Angela Royston, and *The Egg* by Gallimard Jeunesse. Break an egg and let it slide into a saucer. Examine and discuss the different parts of the egg: shell, yolk, and albumen (egg white). Look carefully at the yolk. Near the top is a tiny white spot. That is the part that can grow into a chick. The yolk and white of the egg are the food for the growing chick. The shell is its house.

Egg Sorting

Sort small, medium, and large plastic eggs into small, medium, and large baskets. Label the baskets *small, medium*, and *large*. Sort the eggs into the correct baskets.

Eggshell Garden

Break eggs gently and save the half shells. Save the yolks and egg whites in a separate container. Place the shells in egg cartons and fill them with potting soil. Sprinkle the soil with bird seed. Add water with an eyedropper or a kitchen baster. Place the garden in the sun and water it daily. The seeds will sprout in a few days. Scramble and cook the yolk and egg white for a tasty snack.

Egg Shape Book

Read *What's Hatching Out of That Egg?* by Patricia Lauber. Discuss the different things that could be inside an egg. Use the egg shape template to create an egg shape book. (See figure 4.14.) Illustrate the inside of the egg and write a caption for it.

Chicken Nests

Read and discuss *The Nest* by Brian Wildsmith and *Who Took the Farmer's Hat?* by Joan L. Nodset. Discuss how the nests were made in the stories and create a chicken nest by following the rebus recipe chart. (See figure 4.13.)

Fig. 4.13. Chicken nest.

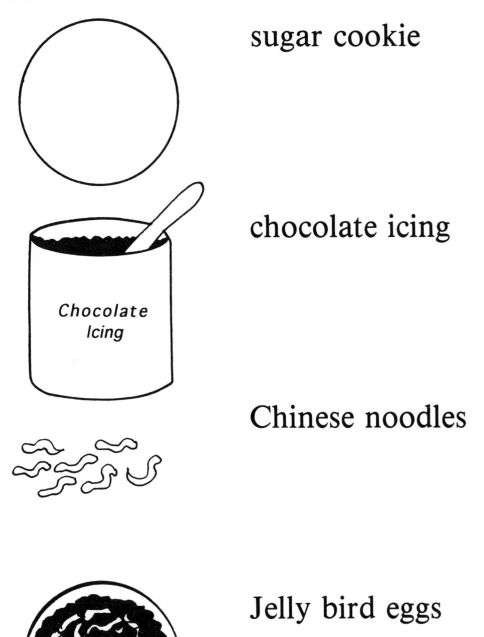

sugar cookie

chocolate icing

Chinese noodles

Jelly bird eggs

Fig. 4.14. Egg shape book directions and pattern.

Materials:

White construction paper
Tagboard template
Markers or crayons
Scissors

What to Do:

Fold paper in half.

Place egg template on fold. Trace and cut out the egg.

Illustrate what's inside your egg.

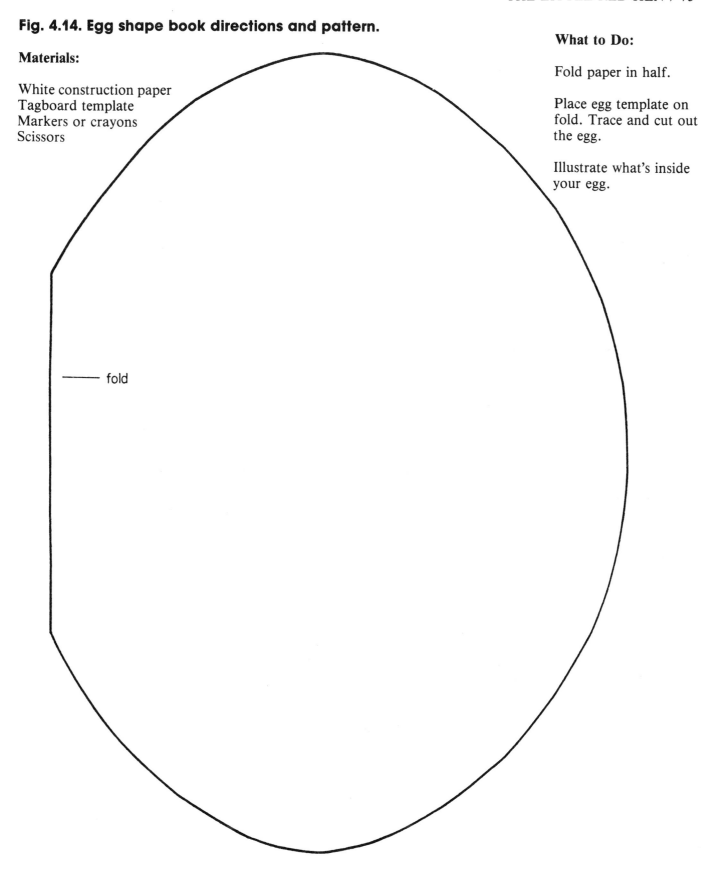

— fold

MUSIC/POETRY/GAME EXPERIENCE

Henny Penny Game

Join hands and walk in a circle around Henny while chanting "Henny Penny."

> Henny over the water,
>
> Henny over the sea.
>
> Henny found a penny
>
> And can't catch me!

Henny picks up the penny from the floor and tags a friend who is walking in the circle. The tagged person becomes Henny, and the game continues until everyone has had a turn being Henny.

Hickety, Pickety Choral Reading

Write "Hickety Pickety" on chart paper and recite it together.

> Hickety, Pickety, my black hen,
>
> She lays eggs for gentlemen;
>
> Gentlemen come every day
>
> To see what my black hen doth lay.

Tell a Tale

Read the following poem, "The Little Hen." Discuss the similarities and differences between it and *The Little Red Hen* book. What do you think the little hen's tale was? Can you tell a tale?

> I had a little hen,
>
> The prettiest ever seen;
>
> She washed the dishes,
>
> And kept the house clean.
>
> She went to the mill
>
> To fetch me some flour,
>
> And always got home
>
> In less than an hour.
>
> She baked me my bread,
>
> She brewed me my ale,
>
> She sat by the fire,
>
> And told a fine tale.

SUPPLEMENTARY COSTUME PIECES

Instructions and a pattern for making the Little Red Hen's comb are in figures 4.15 and 4.16, respectively. Instructions for making cat ears, dog ears, and mouse ears are in figures 4.17, 4.18, and 4.19, respectively.

Fig. 4.15. Little Red Hen comb costume.

Materials:

⅓ yd. of red craft felt
1 orange craft felt square
1 red 42" shoelace

Construction:

- Cut an 18" x 12" rectangle of red felt.

- Use the pattern in figure 4.16 to cut orange felt comb.

- Glue gun comb in place.

- Fold felt and glue gun top.

- Turn inside out (comb will stand up and seam will be hidden).

- Fold up bottom edge 1½" and cut slits ⅛" along fold (see illustration).

- Thread shoelace through slits and gather bottom to measure approximately 10".

- Center shoelace and glue gun it to edge of felt to prevent slipping.

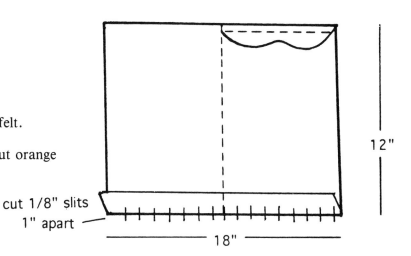

cut 1/8" slits
1" apart

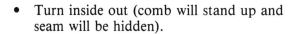

12"

18"

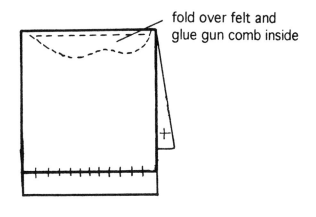

fold over felt and
glue gun comb inside

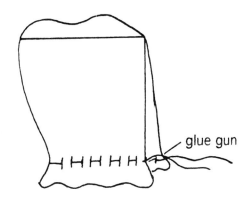

glue gun

Fig. 4.16. Hen comb pattern.

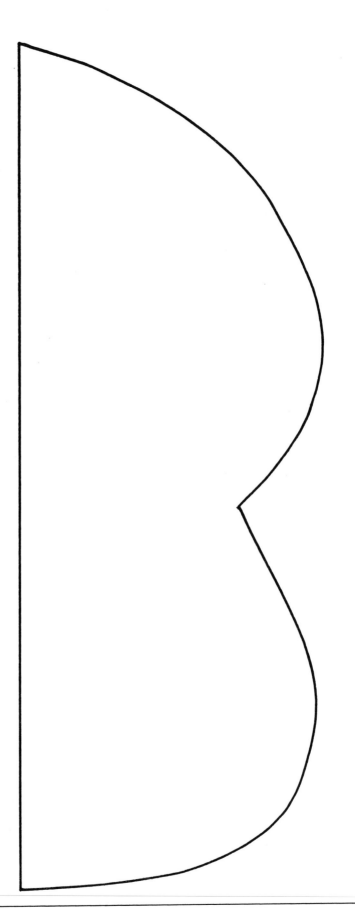

Fig. 4.17. Cat ears.

Materials:

⅛ yd. of yellow craft felt
4" strip of Velcro Sticky Back tape, ¾" wide
Scissors
Pins
Glue gun

Construction:

- Use pattern to cut 2 yellow felt cat ears.

- Cut a 4" x 24" strip of yellow felt for headband.

- Fold headband in half and pin in place.

- Fold ears and glue inside headband.

- Glue gun headband together.

- Glue gun Velcro strips to ends of headband.

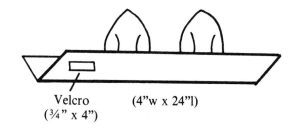

Velcro
(¾" x 4")   (4"w x 24"l)

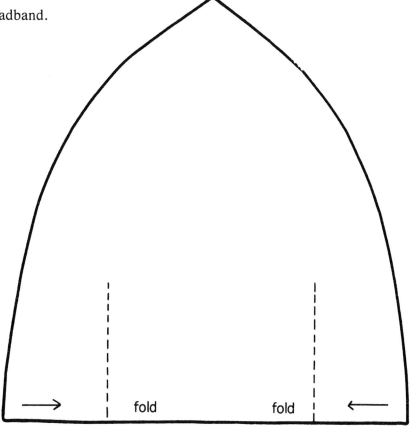

fold   fold

Fig. 4.18. Dog ears.

Materials:

⅛ yd. of tan craft felt
4" strip of Velcro Sticky Back tape, ¾" wide
Scissors
Pins
Glue gun

Velcro
(¾" x 4")

(4"w x 24"l)

Construction:

- Use pattern to cut 2 tan felt dog ears.

- Cut a 4" x 24" strip of tan felt for headband.

- Fold headband in half and pin in place.

- Glue gun ears inside headband (see illustration).

- Glue gun headband together.

- Glue gun Velcro strips to ends of headband.

Fig. 4.19. Mouse ears.

Materials:

⅛ yd. of gray craft felt
1 square of pink craft felt
4" strip of Velcro Sticky Back tape, ¾" wide
Scissors
Pins
Glue gun

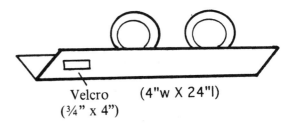

Velcro   (4"w X 24"l)
(¾" x 4")

Construction:

- Use bottom pattern to cut 2 gray felt outer ears.

- Use top pattern to cut 2 pink felt inner ears.

- Cut a 4" x 24" strip of gray felt for headband.

- Fold headband in half and pin in place.

- Glue gun pink inner ear to gray outer ear.

- Glue gun ears inside headband.

- Glue gun headband together.

- Glue gun Velcro strips to ends of headband.

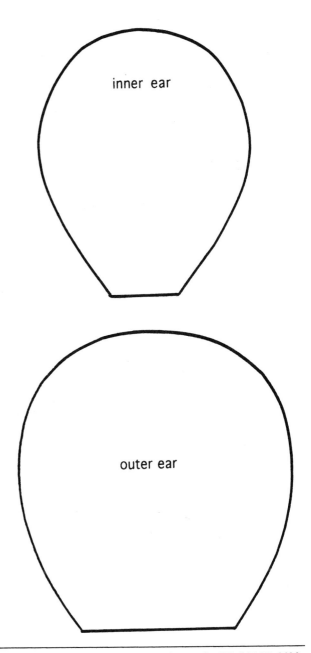

inner ear

outer ear

BIBLIOGRAPHY

The Little Red Hen *Versions*

Berg, Jean H. *Little Red Hen*. Cleveland, OH: Modern Curriculum Press, 1963.

Galdone, Paul. *The Little Red Hen*. New York: Clarion Books, 1973.

Izawa, Tadasu, and Hijkata Izawa. *The Little Red Hen*. New York: G. P. Putnam's Sons, 1981.

McKissack, Patricia, and Frederick McKissack. *The Little Red Hen*. Chicago: Children's Press, 1985.

McQueen, Lucinda. *The Little Red Hen*. New York: Scholastic, 1985.

Schmidt, Karen. *The Little Red Hen*. New York: G & D, 1984.

Southgate, Vera. *The Little Red Hen and the Grains of Wheat*. Auburn, ME: Ladybird Books, 1926.

Stobbs, William. *The Little Red Hen*. New York: Oxford University Press, 1985.

Zemach, Margot. *The Little Red Hen: An Old Story*. New York: Farrar, Straus & Giroux, 1983.

Other Books

Back, Christine, and Jens Olesen. *Chicken and Egg*. Morriston, NJ: Silver Burdett, 1984.

Photographs, drawings, and text follow the development of a chick embryo from the fertilization and laying of the egg to the time the chick hatches.

Dabcovitch, Lydia. *Mrs. Huggins and Her Hen Hannah*. New York: Dutton Children's Books, 1985.

Mrs. Huggins and her hen Hannah did everything together, until one day something happened to change things. A story about the cycle of life.

Demuth, Brennan. *The Ornery Morning*. New York: Dutton Children's Books, 1991.

Farmer Bill wakes up late one morning to discover that all the animals refuse to do their work.

Galdone, Paul. *Henny Penny*. New York: Clarion Books, 1968.

A cumulative nursery tale about a hen who thinks the sky is falling.

_____. *Little Tuppen*. New York: Clarion Books, 1967.

An old Scandinavian nursery tale about a naughty little chicken. A variant of the cumulative folktale pattern.

Heine, Helme. *The Most Wonderful Egg in the World*. London: Picture Lions, 1985.

Three hens quarrel about which one is the most beautiful. The king decides that the one who lays the most beautiful egg will become a princess.

Heller, Ruth. *Chickens Aren't the Only Ones*. New York: Scholastic, 1981.

A book about animals that lay eggs, from chickens to crocodiles.

Hutchins, Pat. *Rosie's Walk*. New York: Scholastic, 1968.
Rosie the hen takes a walk through the farmyard with the fox close behind.

Jeunesse, Gallimard. *The Egg*. New York: Scholastic, 1989.
The illustrations follow a hen's egg from the moment it is laid to the time the chick hatches out. The book also introduces various egg laying animals.

Johnson, Sylvia. *Inside an Egg*. Minneapolis, MN: Lerner Publications, 1982.
Informative book about the inside of an egg.

Kent, Jack. *Little Peep*. New York: Simon & Schuster, 1981.
A comic chain of events featuring a little chicken who thinks his crowing makes the sun come up.

Lauber, Patricia. *What's Hatching Out of That Egg?* New York: Crown, 1979.
Photographs that introduce a variety of eggs and the animals that hatch out of them.

Lobel, Arnold. *How Rooster Saved the Day*. Middlesex, England: Puffin Books, 1981.
A cumulative story about a rooster who outsmarts a robber.

Nodset, Joan L. *Who Took the Farmer's Hat?* New York: Scholastic, 1963.
The farmer's hat is blown away by the wind and ends up as a nest.

Oppenheim, Joanne. *"Not Now!" Said the Cow*. New York: Bantam Books, 1989.
Crow finds a bag of grain and none of the animals will help him plant it. The grain turns out to be popcorn, and he eats it all by himself.

Percy, Graham. *The Cock, the Mouse, and the Little Red Hen*. Cambridge, MA: Candlewick Press, 1992.
The Cock and the Mouse refuse to help the hard working Little Red Hen. When a hungry fox catches them, they regret their laziness.

Turner, Dorothy. *Eggs*. Minneapolis, MN: Carolrhoda Books, 1989.
Clear and concise explanation about eggs.

Wildsmith, Brian. *The Nest*. New York: Oxford University Press, 1987.

Williams, Sue. *I Went Walking*. San Diego, CA: Harcourt Brace Jovanovich, 1989.
A young boy goes for a walk, and a zany parade of colorful animals follows him.

Music

Copus, Pamela, and Joyce Harlow. "Paint With A Feather." *Story Play Music*. Englewood, CO: Teacher Ideas Press, 1992.

CHAPTER
5

THE THREE BILLY GOATS GRUFF

DRAMA/PLAY EXPERIENCE

Introduce the fairy-tale theme with one of the versions of "The Three Billy Goats Gruff." (See bibliography, page 102, for this and other sources.) An excellent one to start with is Janet Stevens's version, in which the smallest billy goat gruff wears a diaper and has a pacifier in his mouth. After reading the story, demonstrate the simpletees costumes and the play props.

Simpletees Costumes

Use simpletees costumes of the three billy goats and the troll for the dramatic play experience. (See figures 5.1 and 5.2.)

Play Props

Construct a troll bridge from a large cardboard box. Paint the box brown. Outline boulders with a black marker. Wear the troll costume and sit under the bridge. Listen for the "trip traps" of the three billy goats. Guess who is trip-trapping over the bridge.

Face Masks

Create face masks of the billy goats and the troll. Use tagboard templates to trace the shapes. (See figures 5.3 and 5.4.)

Stick Puppets/Paper Bag Theater

Make stick puppets of the billy goats and the troll. (See figure 5.5.) Create a paper bag theater for the stick puppets. (See illustration 1.7 on page 8.) Present a play for a friend or take home and present to parents.

Fig. 5.1. Simpletees costumes: The Three Billy Goats Gruff.

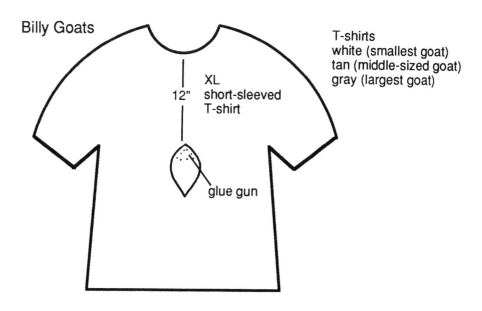

Billy Goats

XL
12" short-sleeved
T-shirt

glue gun

T-shirts
white (smallest goat)
tan (middle-sized goat)
gray (largest goat)

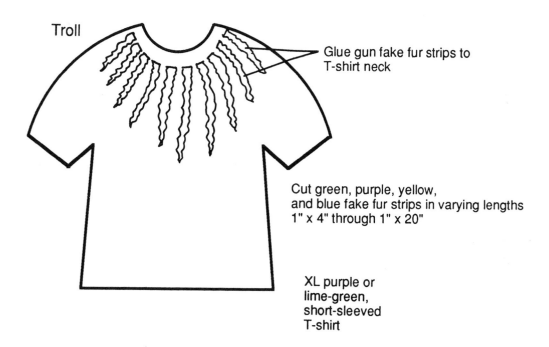

Troll

Glue gun fake fur strips to
T-shirt neck

Cut green, purple, yellow,
and blue fake fur strips in varying lengths
1" x 4" through 1" x 20"

XL purple or
lime-green,
short-sleeved
T-shirt

Fig. 5.2. Goat tail pattern and directions.

Materials:

⅛ yd. of white fake fur
Scissors
Glue gun

What to Do:

Use pattern to cut 3 fur tails (cut on back side).

Glue tails to center back of T-shirts 12" down from the necks.

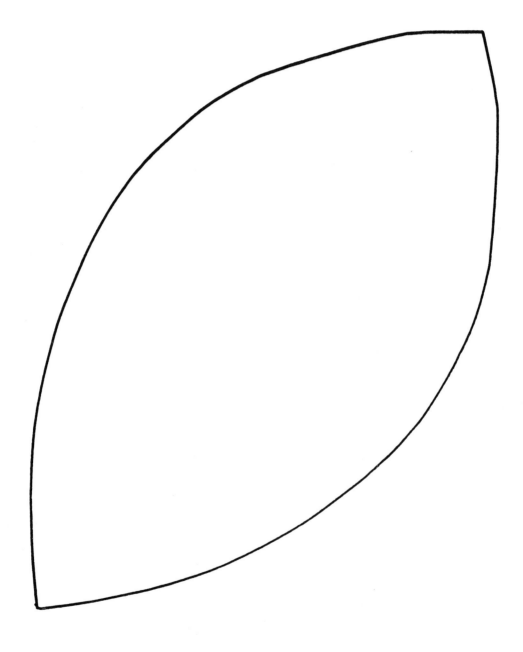

Fig. 5.3. Billy goat face mask pattern.

Fig. 5.4. Troll face mask pattern.

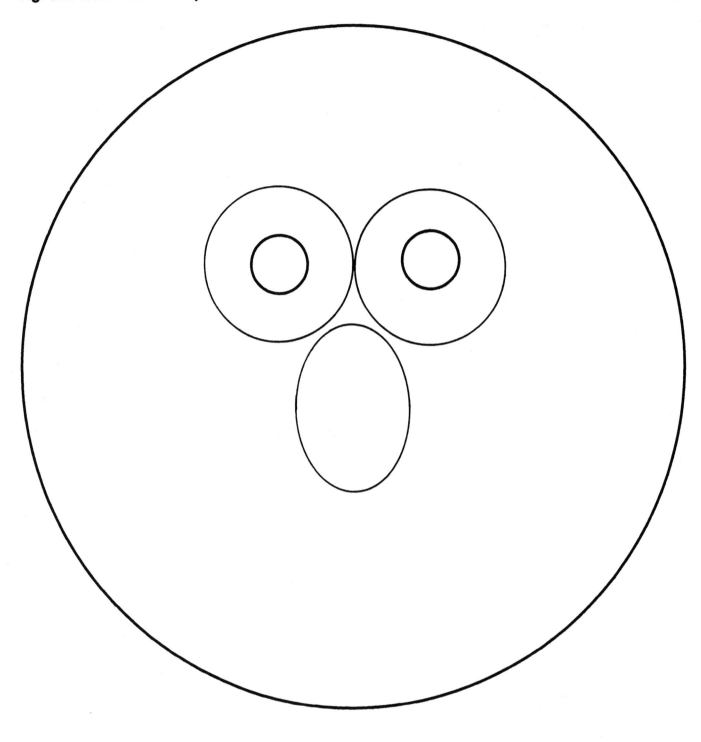

Fig. 5.5. The Three Billy Goats Gruff stick puppet patterns.

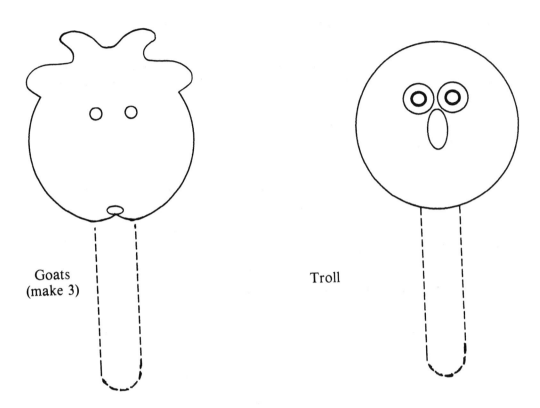

Goats
(make 3)

Troll

LITERATURE/WRITING EXPERIENCE

The Three Billy Goats Gruff *Versions*

Read and discover how versions of "The Three Billy Goats Gruff" differ from each other. Compare the differences between the illustrations. For example, Marcia Brown's billy goats are simple line drawings, while Janet Stevens's billy goats are very detailed, wear clothes, and stand erect.

The Three Billy Goats Gruff *Children's Version*

Write a children's version of "The Three Billy Goats Gruff." Choose a different monster to live under the bridge. Plan a different ending to the story.

Key-Word Books and Key Words

Make a key-word book with the unique or important words in the story. The key words for "The Three Billy Goats Gruff" are as follows:

billy	goat	gruff
grass	troll	over
under	bridge	trip
trap		

Map of the Billy Goats' Journey

Read Olivier Dunrea's *Mogwogs on the March* and Gail Hartman's *As the Crow Flies.* Look at the map of the mogwogs' journey and the animal maps in *As the Crow Flies.* Create a map of the billy goats' journey. Include the valley, the bridge, and the hillside of grass. Add other details to the map. Tell or write about the map.

Goat Shape Book

Make a goat shape book. Trace two goat shapes from tagboard templates. (See figure 5.6.) Illustrate the book and write the story or dictate to the teacher. Use key words for an independent writing experience.

Monster Open-the-Door Book

Read *Maggie and the Monster* by Elizabeth Winthrop. Maggie has a monster that lives behind her door. Make an open-the-door book about the monster. Use markers and draw the monster behind the door. (See figure 5.7.) Tell or write a story about the monster.

Fig. 5.6. Goat shape book directions and pattern.

Materials:

Gray construction
  paper
Tagboard template
White paper
Markers or pencils
Stapler
Key words

What to Do:

Using the tagboard
template, trace and cut
out 2 goat shapes from
gray construction paper.

Teacher may precut
white pages.

Staple the white pages
and cover together at
the top.

Illustrate the book and
write or dictate the
story using key words.

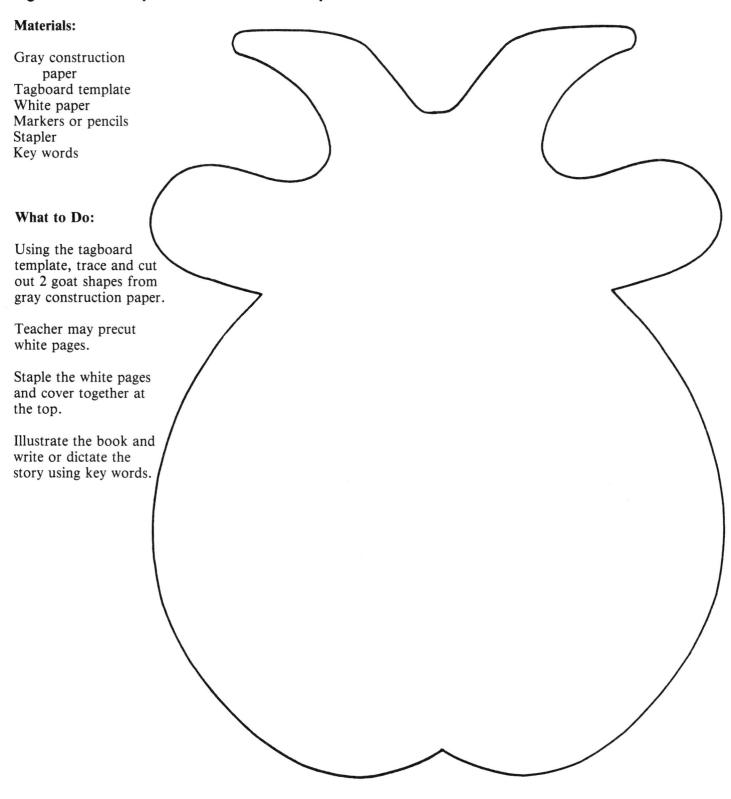

Fig. 5.7. Monster open-the-door book.

Materials:

9" x 12" white construction
    paper
Scissors
Markers or crayons
Glue stick

What to Do:

Fold construction paper in half.

Unfold and fold 1 of the halves in half again.

Cut 2 1½" slits in the fold.

Unfold the paper and cut between the slits to make a door.

Draw a picture of your monster on the uncut side of the paper.

Fold the paper in half again and glue the outside edges together.

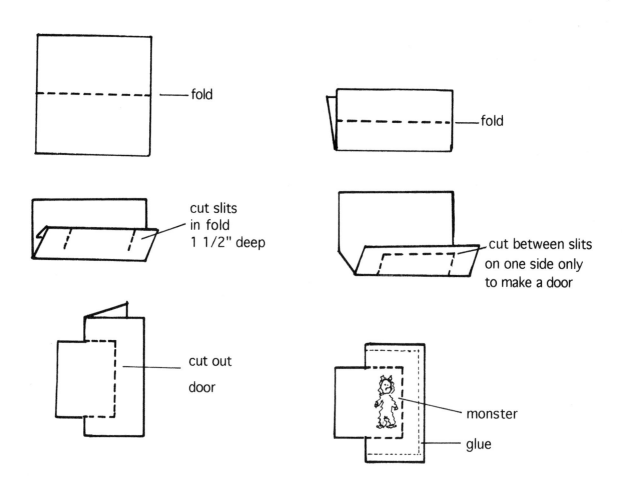

From *Story Play*, copyright 1992. Libraries Unlimited/Teacher Ideas Press, P.O. Box 6633, Englewood, CO 80155-6633.

COOPERATIVE/GROUP EXPERIENCE

Troll Bridge

Construct a troll bridge from a large cardboard box. Paint the box with brown tempera. Use black paint or markers to outline large boulders on the box. Sit under the bridge and listen for the "trip-traps" of the three billy goats gruff.

Troll Parade

Read *Parade* by Donald Crews and *Parade* by Harriet Ziefert. Plan a troll parade. Construct a troll from a brown grocery bag. Stuff the bag with shredded or crumpled paper. Staple the top shut and use markers or paints to make the face. Glue on torn strips of construction paper for the hair. Carry the troll in the troll parade. You can have the parade either indoors or outside.

Troll Obstacle Course

The troll lived *under* the bridge. The goats trip-trapped *over* the bridge. Plan and construct a troll obstacle course with over and under areas. You can build the obstacle course either indoors or outside.

Giant Monster

Read and discuss *Monsters* by Russell Hoban. Use markers or paint to create a giant monster on a long sheet of brown wrapping paper. Work in small groups, each group doing one part of the monster. The finished monster will represent the combined efforts of the groups.

ART/WRITING EXPERIENCE

Tempera Paintings

Read *Monsters* by Russell Hoban and *Maggie and the Monster* by Elizabeth Winthrop. Paint a monster using fluorescent tempera. Write a caption for the painting. Display the paintings on the walls or the bulletin board. Bind the paintings together to make a classroom book.

Saucer Eyes

The troll had "eyes as big as saucers." Make saucer eyes by dipping coffee filters into pans of water mixed with red, yellow, or green food coloring. Allow the saucer eyes to dry overnight. Glue the saucer eyes onto a large sheet of paper. Use markers to make the head and "poker nose."

Salty Names

Gruff was the billy goats' last name. Use a craft stick or your finger to print last names in a tray filled with salt or sand. Copy the names from name tags if necessary. Shake the tray gently to erase the names.

Loom Weaving

Read *The Goat in the Rug* by Charles Blood and Martin Link. Make a weaving like Glenmae did in the book. Use plastic yarn needles, colorful yarn, and rug backing. Rug backing has a large, open weave, and plastic needles threaded with yarn can easily go through it. Rug backing can be purchased in craft stores.

Troll Dolls

Make a troll doll from a clothes pin. Create features with markers. Glue on yarn for the hair and add tiny movable eyes.

Wild Things

Read *Where the Wild Things Are* by Maurice Sendak. Create a wild thing from paper plates and tagboard. Cut shapes from large and small paper plates. (See figure 5.8.) Staple or glue the pieces together. Add features with markers or paint. The teacher may staple the wild things together for younger children.

Fig. 5.8. Wild things directions and patterns.

Materials:

Small and large paper plates
Tagboard
Scissors
Stapler or glue
Markers or paints

What to Do:

Cut paper plates into different shapes (see illustrations).

Staple or glue plate shapes to tagboard.

Use markers or paint to add features.

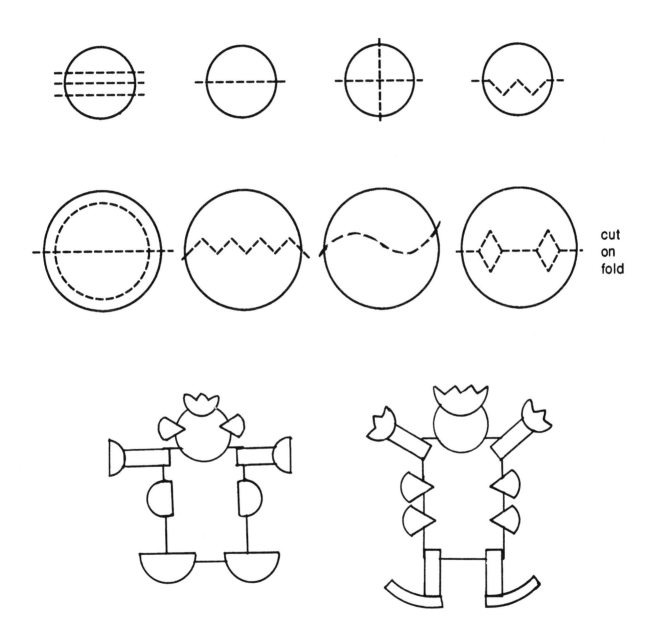

cut
on
fold

COOKING/MATH EXPERIENCE

Cheese Tasting Graph

Taste Swiss, American, and feta, or goat, cheese. Graph everyone's favorite cheese on a simple bar graph. Use cheese wedge cutouts to represent the different cheeses. Compare the results.

Monster Playdough

Create monsters from monster playdough according to the following directions:

Mix together:	1¼ cups flour
	¼ cup salt
	1 package lime Jello™
Stir in:	1 cup boiling water
	1½ tablespoon cooking oil

Knead when cool. Store in a covered container.

Alpha-Bits Names

Use Alpha-Bits cereal to make names. Use name tags if needed. Glue the letters on a card. Repeat as many names as you can find.

Junk Food/Healthy Food

Read and discuss *Gregory, the Terrible Eater* by Mitchell Sharmat. Bring a food item from home. Categorize the items into two groups: healthy food and junk food. Remember that healthy food for people might be junk food for a goat. Decide if your grouping is for goats or people. Categorize the food both ways.

Gruff Gruffs

On a sheet of wax paper, roll one refrigerator biscuit into a long snake. Shape the snake into your last name initial. Lay the initial on a cookie sheet. Brush the initial with melted butter and sprinkle it with a mixture of cinnamon and sugar. Bake as directed on the biscuit can. Use the rebus recipe chart for an independent experience. (See figure 5.9.)

Goat Sorting

Cut out small, medium, and large goats. (See figure 5.10.) Sort the goats into small, medium, and large containers.

Fig. 5.9. Gruff Gruffs.

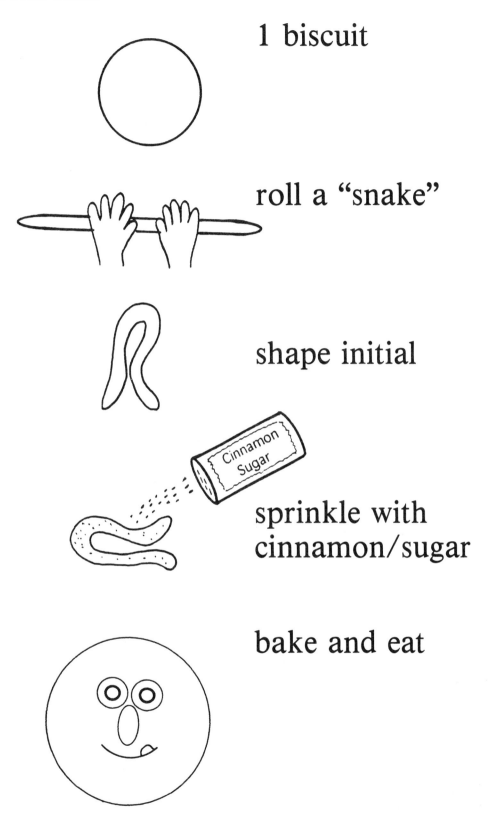

1 biscuit

roll a "snake"

shape initial

sprinkle with cinnamon/sugar

bake and eat

Fig. 5.10. Goat sorting directions and patterns.

Materials:

Gray construction paper
Tagboard and templates
Markers or pencils
Scissors
Small, medium, and
   large containers

What to Do:

Use the templates to
trace small, medium, and
large goats on gray
construction paper.

Sort goats into small,
medium, and large
containers.

Cut out 3 to 5 sets of
goats.

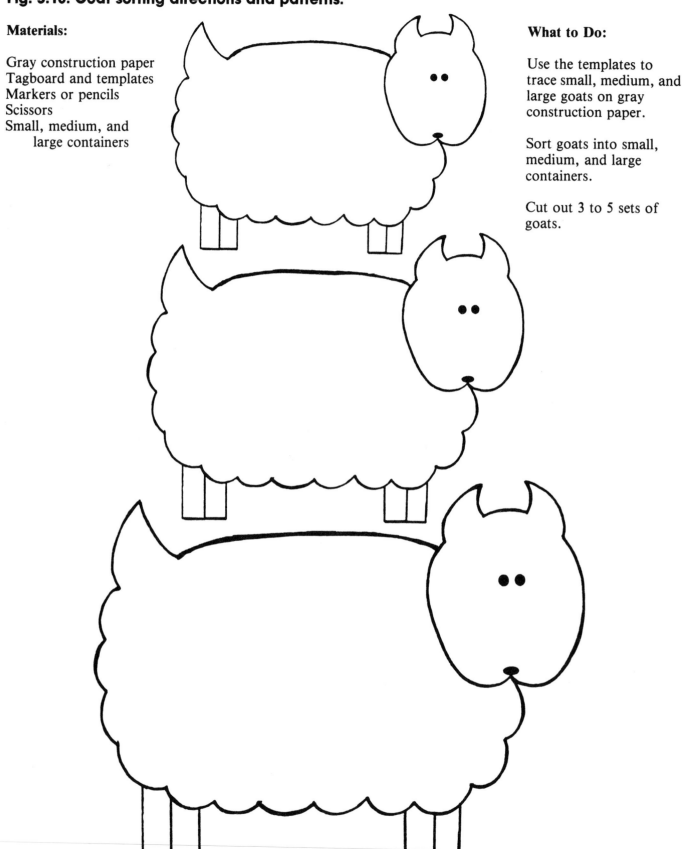

SCIENCE/DISCOVERY EXPERIENCE

Goat Facts

A male goat is called a *billy goat*. A female goat is called a *nanny goat*. A young goat is called a *kid*. Goats are raised for fur, skin, and milk. The milk is used to drink and to make cheese. A goat's tail is short and stands up. Both males and females may have beards under their chins. Goats can find enough food to eat even off of poor land. Goats make good pets.

Goat Grass

Plant rye grass for the billy goats. Fill clear plastic cups with potting soil. Sprinkle rye grass seeds on top of the potting soil. Use an eyedropper or a kitchen baster to squirt water on the seeds. Set the seeds in a sunny window and water them daily. The seeds will sprout in two or three days.

Goat Farm

Visit a goat farm. Milk a goat. Taste goat, or feta, cheese.

Goat Cheese

Let one-half gallon of whole milk stand in an unopened carton until it reaches room temperature. Pour the milk into a large glass bowl and set it in a warm place. Add one-quarter cup of buttermilk to the milk and stir well. Cover the bowl with plastic wrap. Let it sit undisturbed overnight. During the next 24 hours, the milk will become soft. This is called *clabbering*. The watery-looking part is called *whey*, and the solid part is called *curds*. Separate the whey from the curds by pouring it through a strainer or colander. Taste the curds (cheese) and drink the whey.

Curds and Whey

Recite "Little Miss Muffett" and discuss the meanings of *tuffet, curds*, and *whey*.

Little Miss Muffet

Sat on a tuffet

Eating her curds and whey.

Along came a spider

And sat down beside her

And frightened Miss Muffet away.

MUSIC/POETRY/GAME EXPERIENCE

The Name Game

Write your first name on one card and your last name on another card. (The teacher may write names for younger children.) Place the cards in a circle, name side up. Form a circle outside the cards. Call the names of four to six children to walk around looking for their names. When they find their names they pick them up and sit down. Anyone not finding their name sits down empty-handed. Listen to the "Name Game," performed by Pamela Copus, or other good walking music. (See bibliography, page 103.) When the music starts, walk around the cards and look for your first and last names. The music will go from slow to fast. Find your first and last name before the music stops. The game continues until all players have found their names.

The Name Game is similar to Musical Chairs.

Troll Hunt

One child is selected to be "it" and leaves the room. Hide a troll doll in the room. The child who is "it" tries to find the troll doll. Indicate if "it" is close by saying "hot-hot," "warm-warm," or "cold-cold." After finding the troll doll, "it" gets to hide the doll for the next person. Troll dolls can be purchased at most toy stores, or use a clothespin troll doll.

Name Rhymes

Create nonsensical rhymes using your name. For example:

Nicholas, Ticholas	*Michael, Tichael*
Went to the *licholas*	Rode a *bichael*
And had a *picholas*	Took a *hichael*
And soon became *sicholas.*	Found a *nichael*
	Bought a *sichael*
	Wasn't that a *wichael Michael?*

From *Story Play*, copyright 1992. Libraries Unlimited/Teacher Ideas Press, P.O. Box 6633, Englewood, CO 80155-6633.

SUPPLEMENTARY COSTUME PIECES

Instructions for making goat horns are in figure 5.11.

Fig. 5.11. Goat horns.

Materials:

⅛ yd. of gray craft felt
12" strip of Velcro Sticky Back tape, ¾" wide
Scissors
Pins
Glue gun

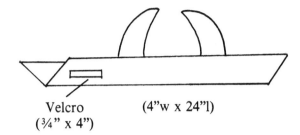

Velcro
(¾" x 4")   (4"w x 24"l)

Construction:

- Use pattern to cut 12 gray felt goat horns.

- Cut 3 4" x 24" strips of gray felt for headbands.

- Fold headbands in half and pin in place.

- Double horns and glue gun together.

- Glue gun horns inside headband (see illustration).

- Glue gun headbands together.

- Cut Velcro into 3 4" strips.

- Glue Velcro strips to ends of headbands.

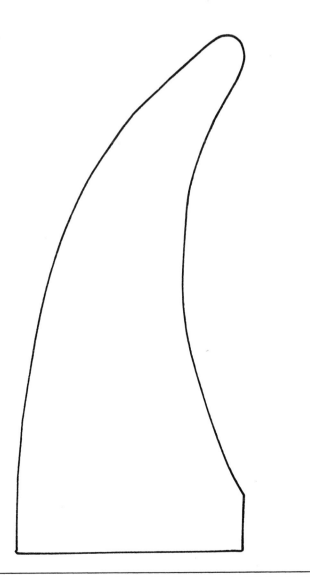

From *Story Play*, copyright 1992. Libraries Unlimited/Teacher Ideas Press, P.O. Box 6633, Englewood, CO 80155-6633.

BIBLIOGRAPHY

The Three Billy Goats Gruff *Versions*

Appleby, Ellen. *The Three Billy Goats Gruff.* New York: Scholastic, 1984.

Asbjornsen, P. C., and J. E. Moe. *The Three Billy Goats Gruff.* San Diego, CA: Harcourt Brace Jovanovich, 1985.

Cosgrove, Stephen. *Billy Goats Gruff.* Nashville, TN: Ideals, 1988.

Galdone, Paul. *The Three Billy Goats Gruff.* New York: Clarion Books, 1973.

Greenway, Jennifer. *The Three Billy Goats Gruff.* Kansas City, MO: Andrews and McMeel, 1991.

Hunia, Fran. *The Three Billy Goats Gruff.* Auburn, ME: Ladybird Books, 1977.

Parker, Ed. *The Billy Goats Gruff.* Mahwah, NJ: Troll Associates, 1979.

Stevens, Janet. *The Three Billy Goats Gruff.* San Diego, CA: Harcourt Brace Jovanovich, 1986.

Other Books

Blood, Charles L., and Martin Link. *The Goat in the Rug.* New York: Macmillan, 1990.
    Geraldine, a goat, describes each step as she and her Navajo friend make a rug, from the hair clipping and carding to the dyeing and actual weaving.

Bolton, Faye. *The Greedy Goat.* New York: Scholastic, 1986.
    The goat was a greedy bully, but the old women found a friend who knew how to get rid of him.

Carle, Eric. *Dragons Dragons and other creatures that never were.* New York: Philomel Books, 1991.
    An illustrated collection of poems about dragons and other fantastic creatures by a variety of authors.

Crews, Donald. *Parade.* New York: Scholastic, 1986.
    Captures the anticipation and excitement of a parade.

dePaola, Tomie. *Helga's Dowry: A Troll Love Story.* San Diego, CA: Harcourt Brace Jovanovich, 1977.
    Helga, a troll, ventures into the world of people to earn her dowry to marry Lars, but things do not work out as she hopes.

Dunn, Judy. *The Little Goat.* New York: Random House, 1978.
    Andy receives a little goat as a birthday present. He names him Sam, and they soon become best friends.

Dunrea, Olivier. *Mogwogs on the March.* New York: Holiday House, 1985.
    The mogwogs march energetically through the countryside until they get tired and go to sleep.

Gackenbach, Dick. *Harry and the Terrible Whatzit*. Boston: Houghton Mifflin, 1977.

When his mother goes to the cellar and doesn't return right away, Harry goes down to search for her and confronts the terrible two-headed whatzit.

Haddock, Peter. *The Wolf and the Seven Kids*. Bridlington, England: Peter Haddock.

A pop-up book about a goat with seven little kids and the wolf who tries to catch them.

Hartman, Gail. *As the Crow Flies: A First Book of Maps*. New York: Bradbury Press, 1991.

Hoban, Russell. *Monsters*. New York: Scholastic, 1989.

John's obsession with drawing monsters results in his being taken to a doctor, where a startling discovery is made about the realism of John's drawings.

Langstaff, John. *Oh, a-Hunting We Will Go*. Boston: Houghton Mifflin, 1974.

"We'll catch a goat and put him in a boat, and then we'll let him go!"

Meyer, Mercer. *Terrible Troll*. New York: Dial Books for Young Readers, 1968.

The imaginary adventures of a small boy and a giant troll.

Peet, Bill. *Jethro and Joel Were a Troll*. Boston: Houghton Mifflin, 1987.

Jethro and Joel, a two-headed troll, go on a rampage through the countryside.

Ross, Tony. *Mrs. Goat and Her Seven Little Kids*. New York: Atheneum, 1990.

Mother Goat rescues six of her kids after they are swallowed by a wicked wolf.

Sendak, Maurice. *Where the Wild Things Are*. New York: Harper & Row, 1963.

Max misbehaves and is sent to his room without any dinner. Magical things happen and he becomes king of the "wild things."

Sharmat, Mitchell. *Gregory, the Terrible Eater*. New York: Scholastic, 1980.

Gregory the goat is not an average goat: he is a terrible eater. His mother and father try to change his eating habits.

Winthrop, Elizabeth. *Maggie and the Monster*. New York: Holiday House, 1987.

Maggie wants to get rid of the monster who visits her room every night and accepts her mother's suggestion to simply ask the monster what it wants.

Ziefert, Harriet. *Parade*. New York: Bantam Books, 1990.

Features the sights, smells, and sounds of the circus parade.

Music

Copus, Pamela, and Joyce Harlow. "The Name Game." *Story Play Music*. Englewood, CO: Teacher Ideas Press, 1992.

CHAPTER
6

JACK AND THE BEANSTALK

DRAMA/PLAY EXPERIENCE

Introduce "Jack and the Beanstalk" by reading one of the versions. (See bibliography, page 119, for this and other sources.) An excellent one to start with is Steven Kellogg's version. The intricate details of the illustrations make this a fascinating picture book. After reading the story, demonstrate the simpletees costumes and the play props.

Simpletees Costumes

Use simpletees costumes of Jack, the mother, the giant, and the giant's wife for a dramatic play experience. (See figure 6.1.) Jack's vest and hat pattern are the same as the woodsman's in chapter 1.

Play Props

Play props can include a treasure chest with coins and jewels, a foam rubber or cardboard ax, plastic eggs, an apron, scarves, a plush hen, an auto harp, a table, and chairs.

Face Masks

Create face masks of Jack, the mother, the giant, and the giant's wife. Use tagboard templates to trace the shapes. (See figures 6.2, 6.3, 6.4, and 6.5.)

Stick Puppets/Paper Bag Theater

Make stick puppets of Jack, the mother, the giant, and the giant's wife. (See figure 6.6.) Create a paper bag theater for the stick puppets. (See figure 1.7 on page 8.) Present "Jack and the Beanstalk" to a friend or take home and present to parents.

Fig. 6.1. Simpletees costumes: Jack and the Beanstalk.

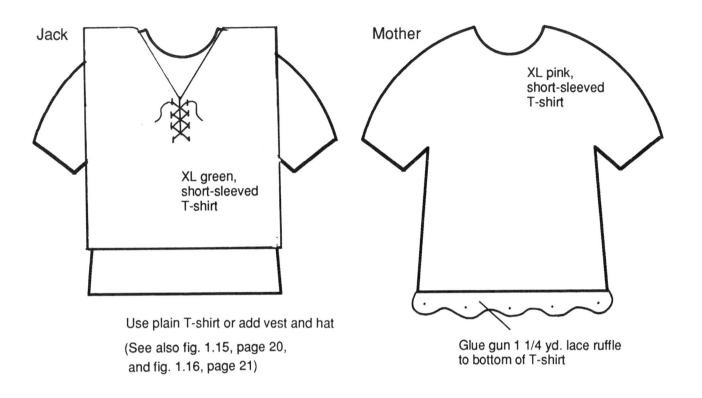

Jack

XL green,
short-sleeved
T-shirt

Use plain T-shirt or add vest and hat

(See also fig. 1.15, page 20,
and fig. 1.16, page 21)

Mother

XL pink,
short-sleeved
T-shirt

Glue gun 1 1/4 yd. lace ruffle
to bottom of T-shirt

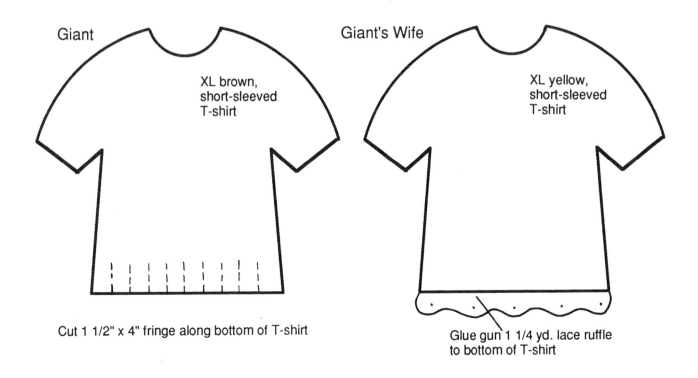

Giant

XL brown,
short-sleeved
T-shirt

Cut 1 1/2" x 4" fringe along bottom of T-shirt

Giant's Wife

XL yellow,
short-sleeved
T-shirt

Glue gun 1 1/4 yd. lace ruffle
to bottom of T-shirt

Fig. 6.2. Jack face mask pattern.

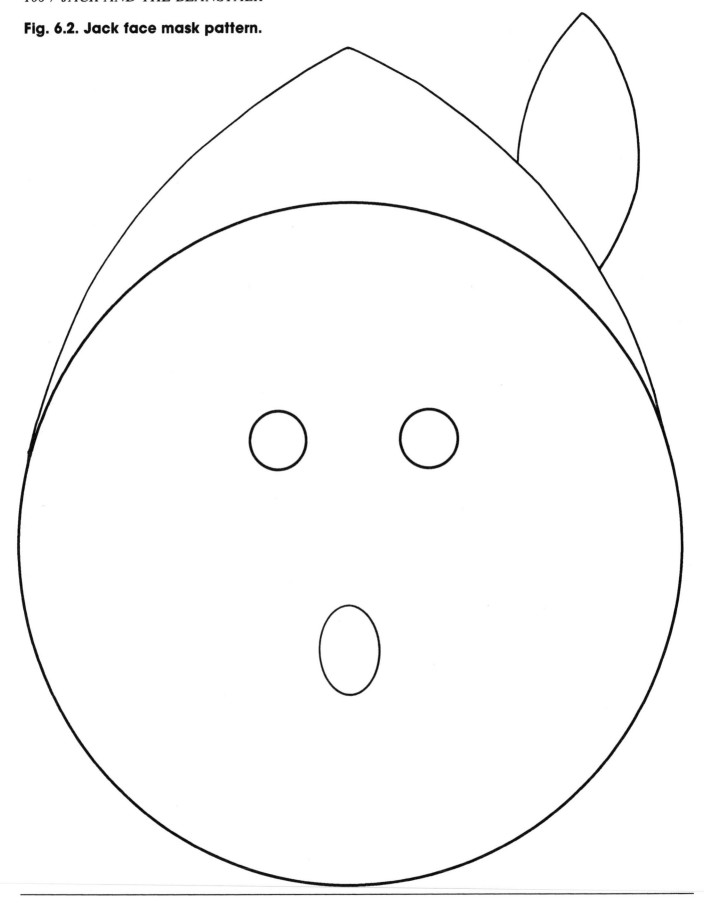

Fig. 6.3. Mother face mask pattern.

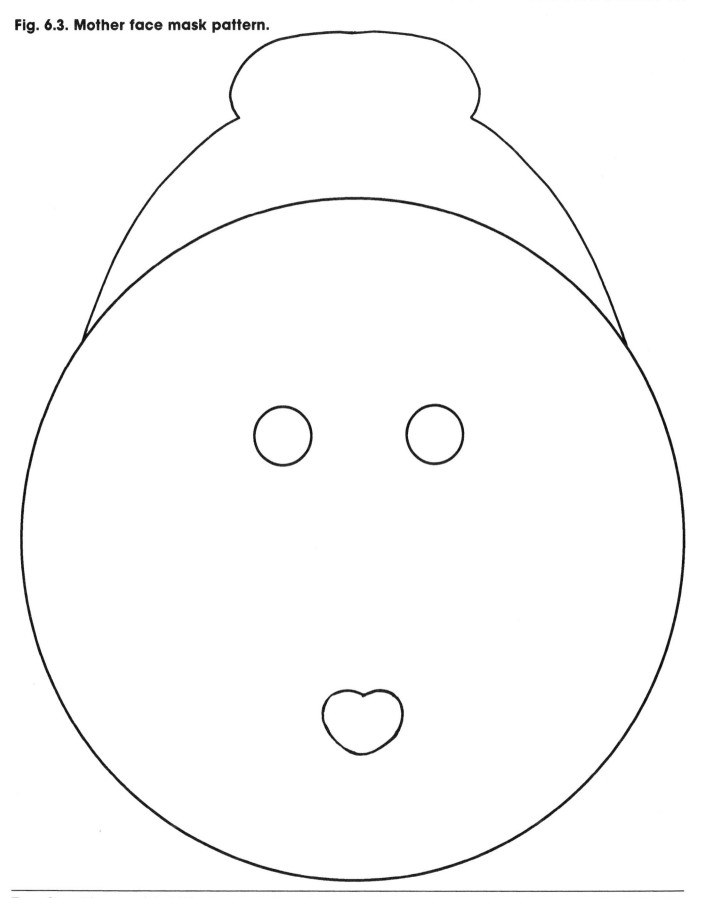

Fig. 6.4. Giant face mask pattern.

Fig. 6.5. Giant's wife face mask pattern.

Fig. 6.6. Jack and the Beanstalk stick puppet patterns.

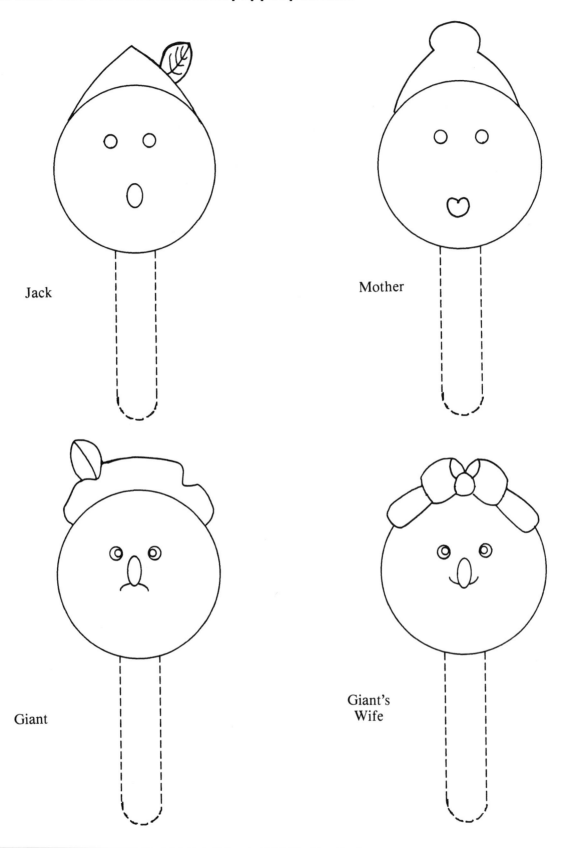

Jack

Mother

Giant

Giant's
Wife

LITERATURE/WRITING EXPERIENCE

Jack and the Beanstalk *Versions*

Read and discover how versions of "Jack and the Beanstalk" differ from each other. Compare the differences in illustrations. For example, Beatrice Schenk de Regniers's and Paul Galdone's versions are told in verse. Steven Kellogg's *Jack and the Beanstalk* is based on the classic version edited by Joseph Jacobs, as it was told to Jacobs in Australia in 1860. Gail E. Haley's *Jack and the Bean Tree* is an Appalachian version.

Jack and the Beanstalk *Children's Version*

Read the giant's account in *Jack and the Beanstalk and the Beanstalk Incident* by Tim Paulson. Write a children's version of "Jack and the Beanstalk." Choose a different ending to the story or choose a different villain.

Key-Word Books and Key Words

Make a key-word book with the unique or important words in the story. The key words for *Jack and the Beanstalk* are as follows:

Jack	magic	bean
mother	cow	hen
harp	giant	beanstalk

Bean Leaf Shape Book

Make a bean leaf shape book by tracing the bean leaf shape from a tagboard template. (See figure 6.7.) Illustrate the book and write a story about Jack or dictate the story to the teacher. Use the key words for an independent writing experience.

Magic Egg Pop-up Book

Make a magic egg pop-up book. (See figure 6.8.) Draw an object to pop up in the egg. Write a caption inside the book.

Fig. 6.7. Bean leaf shape book directions and pattern.

Materials:

Green construction paper
White paper
Tagboard template
Markers or pencils
Stapler
Key words

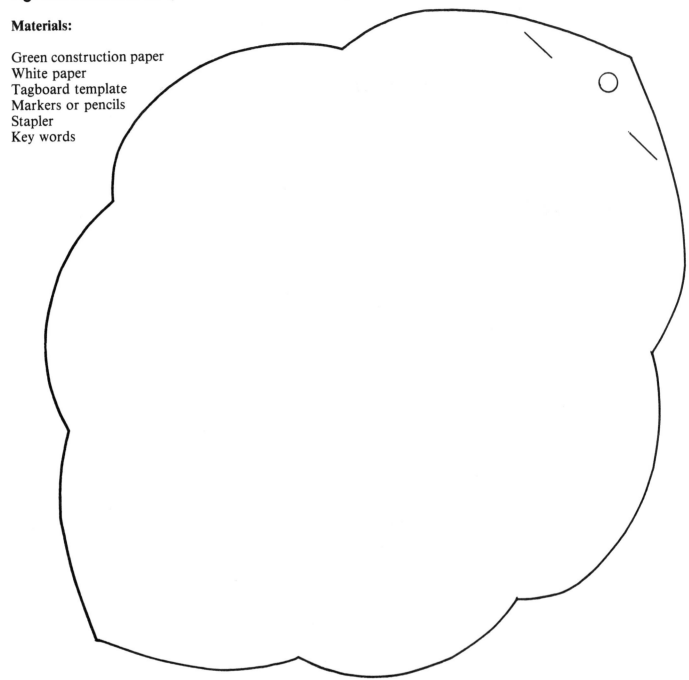

What to Do:

Using the tagboard template, trace and cut out 2 bean leaf shapes from green construction paper.

Teacher may precut the white pages.

Staple the white pages and the cover together.

Illustrate and write a story about Jack.

Use the key words for an independent writing experience.

Fig. 6.8. Magic egg pop-up book directions and pattern.

Materials:

Yellow construction
    paper
Tagboard
Markers or crayons
Scissors

What to Do:

Fold the yellow
construction paper
in half.

Place the egg tem-
plate on the fold
and trace.

Cut out the egg
shape.

Cut 2 parallel lines
on the fold (see
illustration).

Fold the cut strip
back and forth.

Push the strip
through to the
inside.

Draw an object to
pop up from inside
the egg.

Cut out the object
and glue it onto the
pop-up strip.

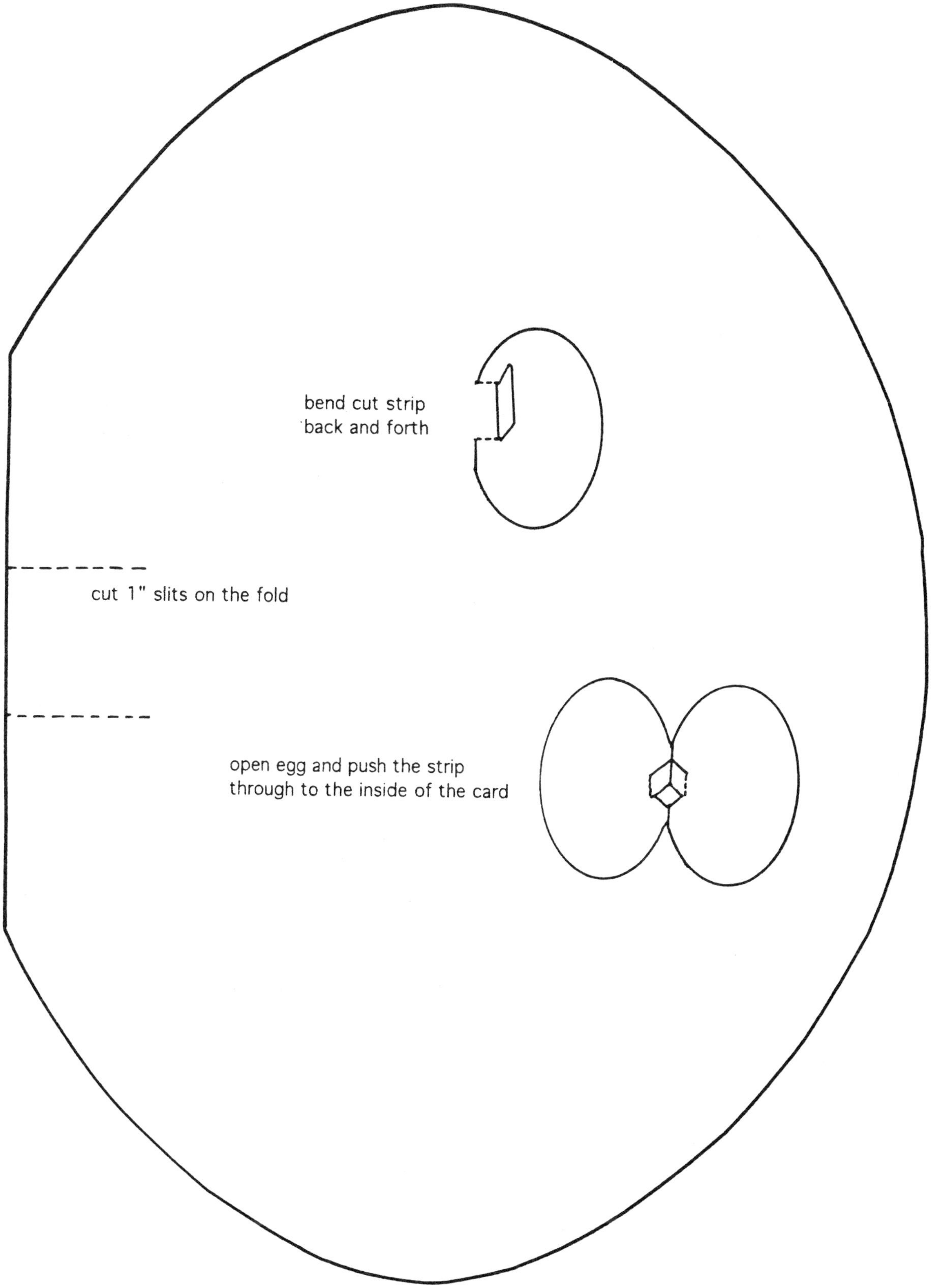

bend cut strip
back and forth

cut 1" slits on the fold

open egg and push the strip
through to the inside of the card

COOPERATIVE/GROUP EXPERIENCE

Beanstalk Mural

Place a long strip of white or brown butcher paper along a wall or on top of a long table. Working in small groups, paint leaves across the paper using three shades of green tempera. (Add blue and yellow to a base green tempera to make other shades of green.) Allow the leaves to dry. Connect the leaves with brown tempera to form a vine. When the beanstalk mural is finished, hang it vertically on a wall.

While painting, play "Fe Fi Fo Fum" (part II), performed by Pamela Copus, or other music. (See bibliography, page 121.)

Pea and Toothpick Structure

Jack is trapped at the top of the beanstalk. Build a structure to help him climb down. Organize the children into small groups to build structures by sticking round toothpicks into dried peas that have been soaked overnight in water. Have successive groups of builders continue to add to the structure. Allow the structure to dry. As the peas dry, they will tighten, and the structure will become strong. Glue on bits of colored art tissue to add detail.

Vine Weaving

Take a ball of brown or green yarn and weave it in and out through the furniture and fixtures in the room. Add leaves to the vine by tying or taping leaves made of green crepe paper or construction paper to the yarn. Add tendrils by tying or taping strips of yarn or crepe paper to the vine.

Jack's Footpath

Jack needs a footpath to help him find his way to the beanstalk. Place a long sheet of white freezer wrap on the floor. Place a flat tray of tempera paint mixed with liquid soap at one end of the paper and a pan of soapy water and a towel at the other end. Step into the tempera paint with bare feet and walk along the paper, leaving your footprints behind. Step into the soapy water at the other end and wash the paint off. Dry your feet with a towel. Use different colors of tempera when more paint is needed. (If you make the footpath outside, you can wash your feet off with a garden hose.) Hang the footpath on a wall.

ART/WRITING EXPERIENCE

Tempera Paintings

In Steven Kellogg's version of "Jack and the Beanstalk" the giant is an ogre. Create your own ogre with fluorescent tempera. Use wild shades of magenta, lime green, and lemon yellow. Write a caption for the ogre painting. Display the paintings on the walls or the bulletin board. Bind the paintings together to make a classroom book.

Bean Collage

Create a collage using an assortment of dried beans. Display the bean collage on the walls or the bulletin boards.

Jack's Clouds

Jack's beanstalk grows so tall that it disappears into the clouds. Read *The Cloud Book* by Tomie dePaola and *Nimby* by Jasper Thompkins. Look at clouds in the sky. Make your own clouds by squirting mounds of shaving cream onto a table top or flat tray. Use your hands and fingers to swirl the clouds over the surface of the table or tray.

COOKING/MATH EXPERIENCE

Measuring and Pouring Beans

Use dried beans such as lima, pinto, red, white, black, and great northern beans. (Beans may be purchased already mixed in the package.) Place the beans in a small tub along with measuring cups, spoons, and funnels. Measure and pour the beans.

Fifteen-Bean Soup

Soak 15-bean soup mix overnight in water. Pour off the soaking water. Add fresh water and cook along with, for example, bacon strips or a ham bone. Bring the beans to a boil and then cook them on low heat for two to three hours (you may use a Crockpot™ or slow cooker). Serve cooked beans for a snack or meal.

Beans-in-a-Pod

Trace two bean pod shapes from a tagboard template. (See figure 6.9.) Staple or glue the bottom edges together. Use a hole punch to punch a hole in one end of the pod. Tie a curled ribbon tendril through the hold. Use dried lima beans to fill the bean pod. Count the beans and write the number of beans on the pod.

Giant's Toe

Read *The Giant's Toe* by Brock Cole. Follow the rebus recipe to make, bake, and eat a giant's toe. (See figure 6.10.) On a sheet of wax paper, roll a refrigerator biscuit into a toe shape. Place the toe on a cookie sheet. Brush the toe with melted butter and sprinkle with a mixture of cinnamon and sugar. Bake the toe according to the package directions and eat it.

Fig. 6.9. Beans-in-a-pod directions and pattern.

Materials:

Green construction paper
Tagboard templates
Markers or pencils
Stapler or glue
Hole punch
Green curling ribbon
Dried lima beans

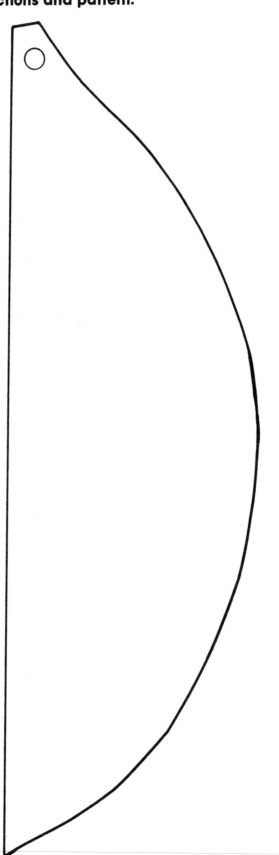

What to Do:

Using the tagboard template, trace 2 bean pod shapes from green construction paper.

Staple or glue the bottom edges together to form a pocket.

Punch a hole in one end of the pod.

Tie a tendril of green curling ribbon through the hole.

Fill the pod with beans.

Count the beans and write the number of beans on the pod.

Fig. 6.10. Giant's toe.

1 biscuit

shape toe

brush butter

sprinkle with
cinnamon/sugar

bake and eat

SCIENCE/DISCOVERY EXPERIENCE

Bean Facts

Beans belong to the pea family. The edible pods and the seeds are both called beans. Some beans grow on bushes, while other beans grow on vines. Beans grow in pods divided lengthwise into two halves. Red kidney beans, pinto beans, and navy beans were first cultivated by the Indians of Central and South America. The lima bean is a large, flat, white or pale green bean. The mung bean is an important food in Asia. Soybeans were cultivated by the Chinese more than 5,000 years ago and probably got their start in Manchuria. There they are called "the meat of the soil." The lentil is the oldest cultivated bean, dating from 8,000 B.C. Its place of origin is southwestern Asia.[1]

Bean Garden

Read *The Tiny Seed* by Eric Carle and *Vegetable Garden* by Douglas Florian. Discuss seeds and how they grow. Place a wet paper towel or wet cotton balls in a plastic sandwich bag, clear plastic cup, or small jar. Add an assortment of beans to the container. Water the beans with an eyedropper or a kitchen baster. Keep the seeds in a dark place for three or four days. Place the bean garden in the sunlight, and in two or three days the beans will begin to sprout.

Bean Sorting and Classifying

Identify and label different kinds of beans. Use an egg carton to sort the beans. Use a package of 15-bean soup mix purchased from a grocery store for the sorting experience.

Mung Bean Sprouts

Place a spoonful of mung beans in a jar. Fill the jar with water and soak the beans overnight. Cover the top of the jar with cheesecloth and fasten the cloth with a rubber band. Drain off the soaking water. Lay the jar on its side in a dark place. Fill the jar with water each day and rinse the sprouts. Pour off the water and return the jar to the dark place. On the fourth day, put the sprouts in a sunny place. The sprouts will start to grow in a few days. Eat the bean sprouts for a snack or sprinkle them on a peanut butter sandwich.

MUSIC/POETRY/GAME EXPERIENCE

Fe Fi Fo Fum

Listen to "Fe Fi Fo Fum" performed by Pamela Copus (bibliography, page 121) while you climb an imaginary beanstalk. Pretend to tiptoe into the castle and listen for the giant, the hen, and the harp. Escape back down the beanstalk when the giant awakens.

---

[1]Sally Stone and Martin Stone. *The Brilliant Bean.* New York: Bantam Books, 1988. Gives the history, origin, and basic facts about 24 different beans from adzuki to winged beans.

Egg Snatcher

Choose one child to be the giant. The giant sits in a chair with his or her back to the children and pretends to be asleep. A plastic egg is placed under the giant's chair. "Jack" is chosen to sneak up, snatch the egg, and hide it underneath his or her legs. The giant is "awakened" by the clucking of the hens (children). The giant has three tries to guess who snatched the egg. Jack then becomes the giant, and the giant chooses a new Jack to snatch the egg. The game continues until all the children have participated.

Jack Be Nimble

Jack must learn how to be nimble and quick to escape from the giant. Discuss and demonstrate the words *nimble* and *quick*. Practice being nimble and quick by jumping over a beanstick. (Use a paper towel roll for the beanstick.) Paint the paper towel roll with brown tempera and glue on a few leaves. Chant the following verse while everyone jumps over the beanstick:

> Jack be nimble
>
> Jack be quick.
>
> Jack jumps over the beanstick.

Giant Steps

Practice making giant steps. Play a giant's version of "Mother May I." Jack is "it" and the other players are the giants. Jack indicates how many giant steps may be taken each turn. The first giant to tag Jack gets to be "it" next. Play the game either indoors or outside.

BIBLIOGRAPHY

Jack and the Beanstalk *Versions*

Burgess, Beverly. *Jack and the Beanstalk.* Tulsa, OK: Harrison House, 1985.

Cauley, Lorinda B. *Jack and the Beanstalk.* New York: G. P. Putnam's Sons, 1983.

de Regniers, Beatrice Schenk. *Jack and the Beanstalk.* New York: Macmillan, 1990.

Faulkner, Matt. *Jack and the Beanstalk.* New York: Scholastic, 1986.

Galdone, Paul. *Jack and the Beanstalk.* New York: Clarion Books, 1974.

Goldsen, Bernette. *Jack and the Beanstalk.* New York: Random House, 1978.

Greenway, Jennifer. *Jack and the Beanstalk.* Kansas City, MO: Ariel Books, 1990.

Hayes, Sarah. *Jack and the Beanstalk.* New York: Crown, 1986.

Howe, John. *Jack and the Beanstalk.* Boston: Little, Brown & Co., 1989.

Kellogg, Steven. *Jack and the Beanstalk.* New York: Morrow Junior Books, 1991.

Paulson, Tim. *Jack and the Beanstalk and the Beanstalk Incident*. New York: Carol, 1990.

Ross, Tony. *Jack and the Beanstalk*. New York: Delacorte, 1981.

Tanner, Suzy Jane. *Jack and the Beanstalk*. New York: Award Publications Limited, 1987.

Other Books

Briggs, Raymond. *Jim and the Beanstalk*. New York: Sandcastle Books, 1970.
     An updated version of the story with a giant who is old and bald, with poor vision and no teeth. Jim solves his problems for him.

Carle, Eric. *The Tiny Seed*. New York: Scholastic, 1987.
     The story of the seasons and a tiny seed that is carried by the wind across an ocean and a desert. The tiny seed grows into a flower and then becomes a seed pod.

Cole, Brock. *The Giant's Toe*. New York: Farrar, Straus & Giroux, 1988.
     A revisionist's version of *Jack and the Beanstalk* that combines reality and whimsy.

Coville, Bruce, and Katherine Coville. *The Foolish Giant*. New York: Harper & Row Junior Books, 1978.
     The adventures of a not very bright but friendly giant named Harry.

dePaola, Tomie. *The Mysterious Giant of Barletta*. San Diego, CA: Harcourt Brace Jovanovich, 1984.
     The giant statue of Barletta is called upon to save the town from an army that is destroying all the towns and cities along the lower Adriatic coast.

_____. *The Cloud Book*. New York: Holiday House, 1975.
     Introduces the ten most common types of clouds, the myths that have been inspired by their shapes, and what they can tell us about coming changes in the weather.

Florian, Douglas. *Vegetable Garden*. San Diego, CA: Harcourt Brace Jovanovich, 1991.
     A family plants a vegetable garden and helps it grow.

Fuchshuber, Annegert. *Giant Story*. Minneapolis, MN: Carolrhoda Books, 1988.
     A lonely dormouse who cannot find a friend and a giant who is an outcast from forest society find solace in each other's company.

Green, Lawrence. *Jack and the Beanstalk*. San Francisco: Visual Impact Designs, 1990.
     A read-a-round book that opens up and unfolds into a three-dimensional toy.

Haley, Gail E. *Jack and the Bean Tree*. New York: Crown, 1986.
     Story dreamers like Poppyseed have been living in the mountains and telling stories about Jack ever since their ancestors brought the stories to the United States from England, Ireland, Scotland, and Germany.

Thompkins, Jasper. *Nimby*. San Diego, CA: Green Tiger Press, 1982.
    An extraordinary cloud meets a remarkable friend.

Music

Copus, Pamela, and Joyce Harlow. "Fe Fi Fo Fum" (Part I & Part II). *Story Play Music.* Englewood, CO: Teacher Ideas Press, 1992.

THE OWL AND THE PUSSYCAT

DRAMA/PLAY EXPERIENCE

Introduce Edward Lear's *The Owl and the Pussycat* by reading the text. (See bibliography, page 138, for this and other sources.) After a courtship voyage of a year and a day, the owl and the pussycat finally buy a ring from Piggy-wig and are blissfully married. After reading the poem, demonstrate the simpletees costumes and the play props.

Simpletees Costumes

Use simpletees costumes of the owl, the pussycat, Piggy-wig, and the turkey for a dramatic play experience. (See figures 7.1, 7.2, 7.3, and 7.4.) (A cat ears pattern is in figure 4.17, page 79.)

Play Props

Play props can include a treasure chest with shillings and other play money, a small picnic basket with a large cloth napkin and a tea set, a plastic jar of honey, a runcible spoon, a guitar, and a large cardboard box for a boat.

Face Masks

Create face masks of the owl, the pussycat, Piggy-wig, and the turkey. Use tagboard templates to trace the different characters. (See figures 7.5, 7.6, 7.7, and 7.8.)

Stick Puppets/Paper Bag Theater

Make stick puppets of the owl, the pussycat, Piggy-wig, and the turkey. (See figure 7.9.) Create a paper bag theater for the stick puppets. (See figure 1.7, on page 8.) Present *The Owl and the Pussycat* to a friend or take home and present to parents.

Fig. 7.1. Simpletees costumes: *The Owl and the Pussycat.*

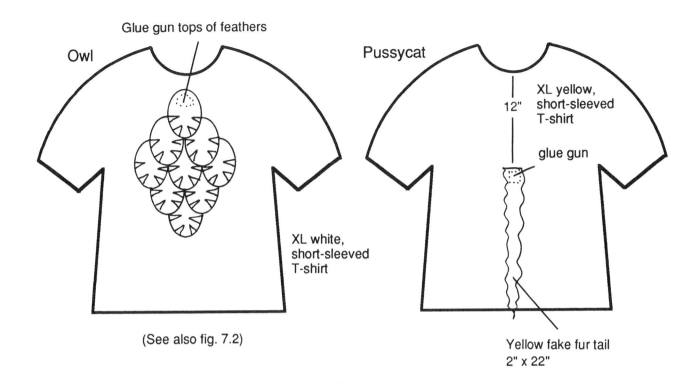

Owl

Glue gun tops of feathers

XL white,
short-sleeved
T-shirt

(See also fig. 7.2)

Pussycat

12" XL yellow,
short-sleeved
T-shirt

glue gun

Yellow fake fur tail
2" x 22"

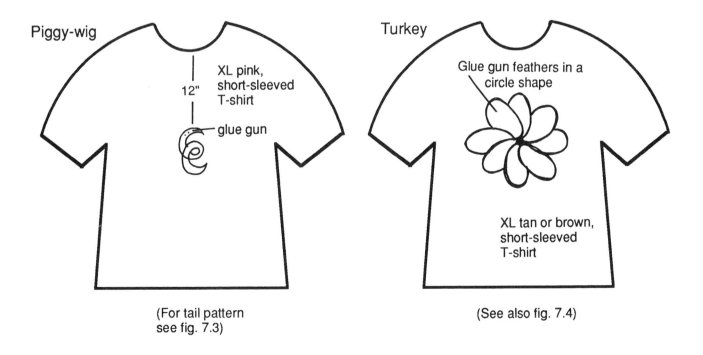

Piggy-wig

12" XL pink,
short-sleeved
T-shirt

glue gun

(For tail pattern
see fig. 7.3)

Turkey

Glue gun feathers in a
circle shape

XL tan or brown,
short-sleeved
T-shirt

(See also fig. 7.4)

Fig. 7.2. Owl feather pattern and directions.

Materials:

⅛ yd. of gray craft felt
Scissors
Pins
Glue gun

Construction:

- Use pattern to cut 9 felt feathers.

- Glue tops of feathers to back of white T-shirt

- Overlap feathers in diamond shape.

Fig. 7.3. Piggy-wig tail pattern and directions.

Materials:

Pink craft felt square
Scissors
Glue gun

Construction:

- Use pattern to cut 2 felt pig tails.

- Double tails and glue gun together.

- Glue gun top of tail 12" down from neck of T-shirt.

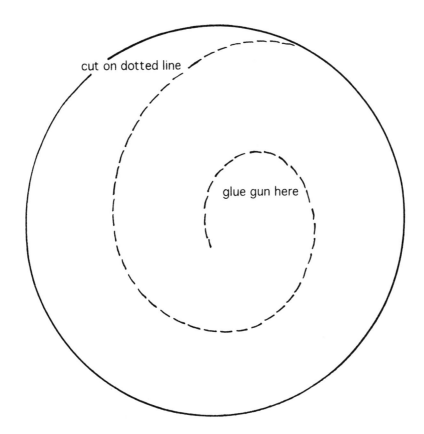

cut on dotted line

glue gun here

Fig. 7.4. Turkey feather pattern and directions.

Materials:

⅛ yd. of orange craft felt
Scissors
Pins
Glue gun

Construction:

- Use pattern to cut 8 felt feathers.

- Glue gun tops of feathers to back of T-shirt.

- Overlap feathers in circle shape.

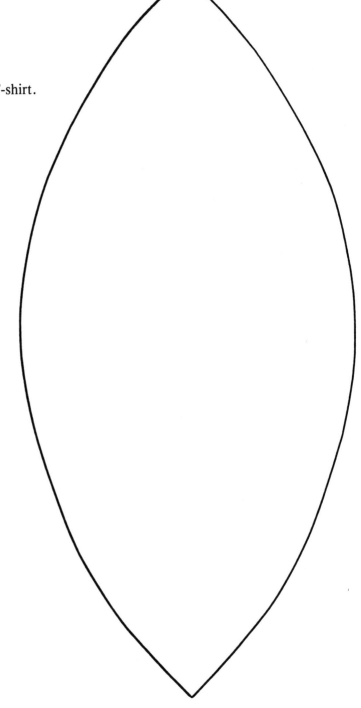

Fig. 7.5. Owl face mask pattern.

Fig. 7.6. Pussycat face mask pattern.

Fig. 7.7. Piggy-wig face mask pattern.

Fig. 7.8. Turkey face mask pattern.

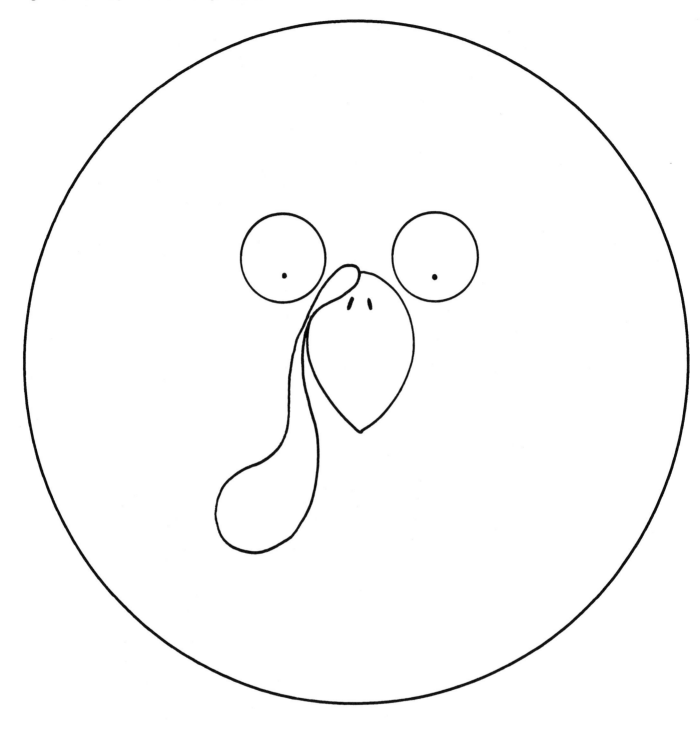

Fig. 7.9. *The Owl and the Pussycat* **stick puppet patterns.**

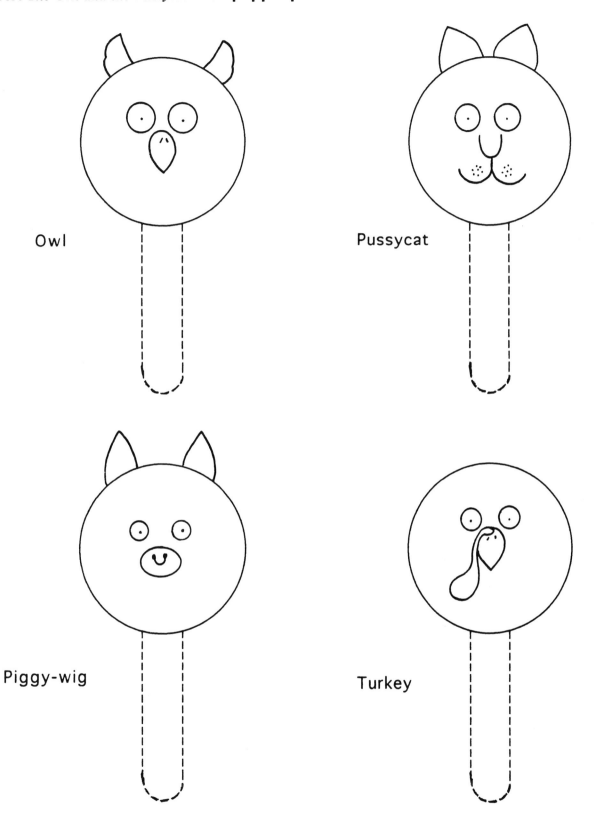

Owl

Pussycat

Piggy-wig

Turkey

LITERATURE/WRITING EXPERIENCE

The Owl and the Pussycat *Versions*

Read different versions of *The Owl and the Pussycat* and compare the illustrations. For example, Louise Voce's illustrations are cartoonlike, while Helen Cooper's characters are lifelike. Jan Brett sets her version in the Caribbean with tropical skies and a fascinating underwater seascape.

The Owl and the Pussycat *Children's Version*

Write a children's version of *The Owl and the Pussycat* on a large sheet of chart paper.

Key-Word Books and Key Words

Make a key-word book with the unique or important words from the poem. The key words for *The Owl and the Pussycat* are as follows:

owl	pussycat	Piggy-wig
turkey	Bong-tree	guitar
honey	money	ring
mince	quince	runcible spoon
moon		

Wedding Invitations

Design and write invitations to the owl and the pussycat's wedding. For example:

You are invited to a wedding

on Bong-tree Island.

Dinner with a runcible spoon

and dancing by the light of the moon.

Owl Shape Book

Make an owl shape book by tracing the owl shape from a tagboard template. (See figure 7.10.) Illustrate the book and write the story or dictate it to the teacher. Use the key words for an independent writing experience.

Fig. 7.10. Owl shape book directions and pattern.

Materials:

Gray construction paper
Tagboard template
White paper
Markers or pencils
Stapler
Key words

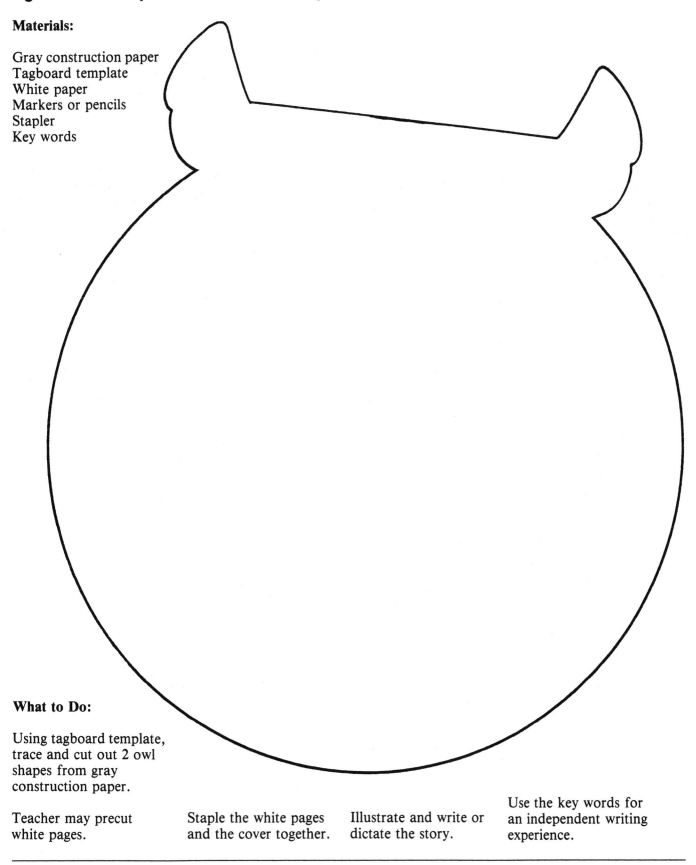

What to Do:

Using tagboard template, trace and cut out 2 owl shapes from gray construction paper.

Teacher may precut white pages.

Staple the white pages and the cover together.

Illustrate and write or dictate the story.

Use the key words for an independent writing experience.

COOPERATIVE/GROUP EXPERIENCE

Pea-Green Boat

Working in small groups, paint a large, flat, rectangular box pea green. The box should be large enough for two children to sit in. Mix yellow tempera with green tempera to get a pea-green shade. Use a large dowel rod and white paper to make a sail for the boat. Use the finished boat in the dramatic play center.

Life Cycle of the Bong-tree

Read *Whisper from the Woods* by Victoria Wirth. The book portrays the life cycle of a forest. Discuss the life cycle of a Bong-tree. Working in small groups, illustrate on large sheets of paper the different stages in the life cycle of a Bong-tree. Write captions for each cycle and display the pictures on the walls or the bulletin board. Bind the drawings together to make a book. Read books about other unusual trees, such as *The Lorax* by Dr. Seuss and the story of the baobab tree in *Tree of Life* by Barbara Bash.

Bark Rubbings

Read *Once There Was a Tree* by Natalia Romanova and *The Tree* by Gallimard Jeunesse. The trees belong to everyone, because they grow from the earth, which is home to all of us. Examine a tree's bark with a magnifying glass. Feel the texture of the bark and smell the tree. Mark bark rubbings from trees. Use brown wrapping paper and a black crayon with the paper peeled off. Work in groups of two, with one person holding the paper against the tree and one person rubbing with the side of the crayon. Share your rubbings with the class.

ART/WRITING EXPERIENCE

Tempera Paintings

Paint a picture of the owl and the pussycat with the pea-green boat. Use gray, yellow, blue, and pea-green tempera. Mix yellow tempera with a base green color to get a pea-green shade. Mix a small amount of black tempera with white base to get a gray shade. Write a caption for the painting. Display the paintings on the walls or the bulletin board. Bind the paintings together to make a classroom book.

Bong-tree Painting

Use sponges cut into leaf shapes to paint the imaginary Bong-tree on a large sheet of paper. A pattern for a Bong-tree leaf is in figure 7.11. Use shades of magenta, lime green, and lemon yellow fluorescent paint to make the leaves. Use black or brown tempera and thin, rectangular sponges to make the trunk and branches. Display the paintings on the walls to create a Bong-tree jungle.

The painting may be accompanied by "The Bong Tree," performed by Pamela Copus, or by other music. (See bibliography, page 140.)

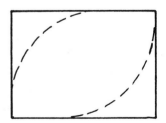

Fig 7.11.
Bong-tree leaf pattern.

Seashell Collage

Glue shell macaroni onto a sheet of white construction paper. Allow the collage to dry overnight. Brush a thin layer of blue tempera or watercolor across the shells. Display the collages on the walls or the bulletin board.

COOKING/MATH EXPERIENCE

Banana Boat

Make a banana boat. Cut a banana in half lengthwise. Use a toothpick and a large marshmallow to make the sail. Eat the boat.

Heart Sandwich

The owl gave his heart to the pussycat. Cut a slice of white bread with a heart-shaped cookie cutter. Spread softened cream cheese mixed with shredded pineapple on the heart-shaped bread. Share your heart and enjoy.

Melting Moments

Celebrate the owl and the pussycat falling in love with Melting Moments.

Combine:	1 cup softened margarine
	⅓ cup sifted confectioners' sugar
Add:	⅔ cup cornstarch
	1 cup all-purpose flour

Chill dough for approximately 1 hour. Form into small balls and place on a cookie sheet. Bake at 350° for 15 minutes.

Pussycat Face Cookies

Make a pussycat face cookie by following the rebus recipe. (See figure 7.12.) Use yellow food coloring to tint coconut for the fur. Use a sugar cookie for the base and ice it with prepared white icing. Sprinkle yellow coconut on the white icing. Use two red hots for the eyes.

Fig. 7.12. Pussycat face cookie.

1 sugar cookie

spread icing

sprinkle coconut

add 2 red hots

enjoy

SCIENCE/DISCOVERY EXPERIENCE

Owl Facts

The barn owl has superb hearing and can hear the minute squeaks and rustles of field mice. An owl's diet consists of mice, voles, rats, sparrows, bats, frogs, and large insects. The barn owl has large eyes and feathers that are soft and fluffy. The soft feathers help muffle the sound of the owl's flight so that its prey is unaware of its approach. Owls are useful to farmers because they destroy harmful rodents. Barn owls mate for life. The female lays four to seven eggs at a time. Both the male and the female help take care of the eggs and the owlets.

Shell Collections

Display collections of seashells. Use field guidebooks to help identify the seashells. Two excellent guides for children are *Seashells of the World* by Tucker Abbot and *Seashores* by Herbert S. Zim.

Fish Observation

Observe a goldfish. A goldfish makes an excellent pet for the classroom. In Jan Brett's illustrations of *The Owl and the Pussycat*, a yellow fish has its own adventure at the bottom of the pages. Read *The Underwater Alphabet Book* by Jerry Pallotta to see some more exotic fish.

Sand Casting

Put 2 to 3 inches of sand in the bottom of a flat tray. Sprinkle water on the sand to make it damp. Press seashells into the sand, then lift them off and examine the prints they have made.

MUSIC/POETRY/GAME EXPERIENCE

The Whooo Game

Read *Good Night Owl* by Pat Hutchins. The owl can't sleep because of all the noise the other animals make. To play the Whooo Game, choose one child to be the pussycat. The pussycat sits in a chair with his or her back to the class. An owl is chosen and leaves the room. The owl calls "whooo" to the pussycat, who must guess the owl's identity. Continue the game until all have participated. This game is similar to "Policeman, Policeman."

Boats Sailing

Two children hold hands and go around in a circle while the remaining children sing "Boats Sailing":

(Tune: "Someone's in the Kitchen with Dinah")

Boats sailing over the ocean.

Boats sailing over the sea.

Boats sailing over the ocean.

Wait a minute, don't leave me.

At the end of the song, the two children drop hands and pick two more children to join the circle. Continue until everyone is in the circle.

Bobby Shaftoe Choral Reading

Recite "Bobby Shaftoe":

Bobby Shaftoe's gone to sea,

Silver buckles at his knee:

He'll come back and marry me,

Bonny Bobby Shaftoe.

Bobby Shaftoe's bright and fair,

Combing down his yellow hair,

He's mine for evermore,

Bonny Bobby Shaftoe.

BIBLIOGRAPHY

The Owl and the Pussycat

Lear, Edward. *The Owl and the Pussycat.* Illustrated by Jan Brett. New York: G. P. Putnam's Sons, 1991.

_____. *The Owl and the Pussycat.* Illustrated by Lorinda Bryan Cauley. New York: G. P. Putnam's Sons, 1986.

_____. *The Owl and the Pussycat.* Illustrated by Helen Cooper. New York: Dial Books for Young Readers, 1991.

_____. *The Owl and the Pussycat.* Illustrated by Paul Galdone. Boston: Houghton Mifflin, 1987.

_____. *The Owl and the Pussycat.* Illustrated by Janet Stevens. New York: Holiday House, 1983.

_____. *The Owl and the Pussycat.* Illustrated by Louise Voce. New York: Lothrop, Lee & Shepard Books, 1991.

Other Books

Abbot, Tucker R. *Seashells of the World*. New York: Golden Press, 1985.
A guide and information to the world of marine seashells.

Bailey, Jill. *Life Cycle of an Owl*. New York: Franklin Watts, 1990.
Nonfiction book about an owl's life cycle.

Bash, Barbara. *Tree of Life: The World of the African Baobab*. Boston: Little, Brown & Co., 1989.
The story of Africa's baobab tree.

dePaola, Tomie. *Tomie dePaola's Mother Goose*. New York: G. P. Putnam's Sons, 1985.
An illustrated collection of over 200 Mother Goose nursery rhymes.

Hutchins, Pat. *The Surprise Party*. New York: Macmillan, 1969.
A funny, cumulative tale about a surprise party.

_____. *Good Night Owl*. New York: Macmillan, 1972.
A cumulative story about an owl who can't sleep because of all the noise the other animals are making.

Jeunesse, Gallimard. *The Tree*. New York: Scholastic, 1992.
The life cycle of a tree from seed to maturity.

Pallotta, Jerry. *The Underwater Alphabet Book*. Watertown, MA: Charlesbridge, 1991.
Features a different fish for each letter of the alphabet.

Romanova, Natalia. *Once There Was a Tree*. New York: Dial Books for Young Readers, 1985.
The life cycle of a tree and the many animals that lay claim to it.

Satoru, Sato. *I Wish I Had a Big, Big Tree*. New York: Lothrop, Lee & Shepard, 1971.
A boy imagines he has a gigantic tree.

Seuss, Dr. *The Lorax*. New York: Random House, 1991.
The forest was once beautiful, but someone is destroying all the trufulla trees.

Thaler, Mike. *Owly*. New York: Harper & Row, 1982.
When Owly asks his mother question after question about the world, she finds just the right ways to help him find the answers.

Wirth, Victoria. *Whisper from the Woods*. New York: Simon & Schuster, 1991.
A poetic portrayal of the life cycle of a forest as the trees share their thoughts and wisdom over the years.

Yolen, Jane. *Owl Moon*. New York: Scholastic, 1987.
A small child goes owling with his Pa on a cold winter's night.

Zim, Herbert S. *Seashores.* New York: Golden Press, 1955.
    A guide to animals and plants along the beaches.

Music

Copus, Pamela, and Joyce Harlow. "The Bong Tree." *Story Play Music.* Englewood, CO: Teacher Ideas Press, 1992.

THREE BLIND MICE

DRAMA/PLAY EXPERIENCE

Discover the complete story of the *Three Blind Mice* as written by John W. Ivimey. Different editions are illustrated by Lorinda Bryan Cauley, Victoria Chess, and Paul Galdone. (See bibliography, page 155, for this and other sources.) Demonstrate the play props and the simpletees costumes of the three blind mice and the farmer's wife.

Simpletees Costumes

Use simpletees costumes of the three mice and the farmer's wife for a dramatic play experience. (See figure 8.1.) For the mouse ears pattern and directions, see figure 4.19 on page 81.

Play Props

Play props can include mouse food, such as plastic ears of corn, and three scarves for blindfolds. Add a doctor's or nurse's kit and include a plastic bottle of Never Too Late to Mend medicine. Also include a small apron, a large pretend knife, and an unbreakable mirror.

Face Masks

Create face masks of the three mice and the farmer's wife. Use tagboard templates to trace the shapes. (See figures 8.2 and 8.3.)

Stick Puppets/Paper Bag Theater

Make stick puppets of the three mice and the farmer's wife. (See figure 8.4.) Create a paper bag theater for the stick puppets. (See figure 1.7 on page 8.) Present the *Three Blind Mice* to a friend or take home and present to parents.

Fig. 8.1. Simpletees costumes: *Three Blind Mice.*

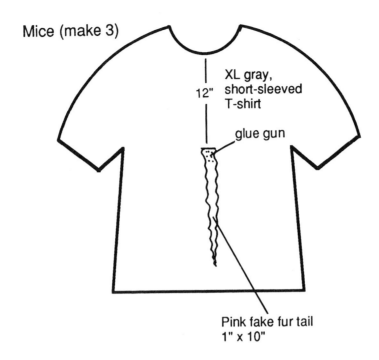

Mice (make 3)

12"

XL gray,
short-sleeved
T-shirt

glue gun

Pink fake fur tail
1" x 10"

Farmer's Wife

XL pink,
short-sleeved
T-shirt

Glue gun 1 1/4 yd. lace ruffle
to bottom of T-shirt

Fig. 8.2. Blind mice face mask pattern.

Fig. 8.3. Farmer's wife face mask pattern.

Fig. 8.4. *Three Blind Mice* **stick puppet patterns.**

Mice
(make 3)

Farmer's Wife

LITERATURE/WRITING EXPERIENCE

Three Blind Mice *Versions*

Discover how different illustrators interpret the *Three Blind Mice*. For example, Lorinda Bryan Cauley's mice open a pastry shop at the end of the story, while Victoria Chess's mice open a strawberry jam shop.

Three Blind Mice *Children's Version*

Use a large sheet of chart paper to write the children's version of the end of the *Three Blind Mice*. Perhaps the mice open a cheese shop or a bookstore. Maybe they decide to take a vacation.

Key-Word Books and Key Words

Make a key-word book with the unique or the important words from the poem. The key words for *Three Blind Mice* are as follows:

three	blind	mice
farmer	wife	carving
eyes	knife	cut
tails		

Diary of a Mouse

Read *A Mouse's Diary* by Michelle Cartlidge or *Diary of a Victorian Mouse* by Angel Dominquez. Pretend to be a mouse and keep a record of a day or a week's activities. Diaries may be kept individually or by small groups.

Braille Books

Discover books in braille. Invite a visually impaired person to talk to the class and explain how he or she compensates for not having sight.

Mouse Cookbook

Write or dictate a mouse recipe. Complete the sentence, "If I were a mouse, my favorite food would be _____." Illustrate the mouse recipe. Bind recipes together to make a classroom cookbook.

Mouse Shape Book

Make a mouse shape book (see fig. 8.5). Trace and cut out two mouse shapes from a tagboard template. Illustrate the book and write the story or dictate it to the teacher. Use key words for an independent writing experience.

Fig. 8.5. Mouse shape book directions and pattern.

Materials:

Gray construction paper
Tagboard template
White paper
Markers or pencils
Scissors
Stapler
Key words

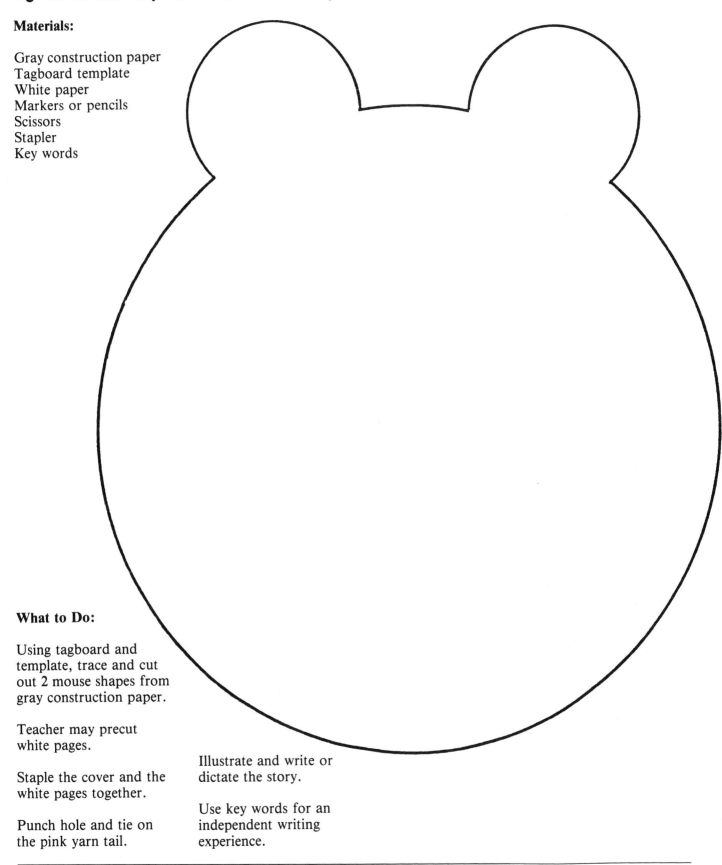

What to Do:

Using tagboard and template, trace and cut out 2 mouse shapes from gray construction paper.

Teacher may precut white pages.

Staple the cover and the white pages together.

Punch hole and tie on the pink yarn tail.

Illustrate and write or dictate the story.

Use key words for an independent writing experience.

COOPERATIVE/GROUP EXPERIENCE

Where's Mouse?

Read *Where Are You Going, Little Mouse?* by Robert Kraus and *Where's Waldo?* by Martin Handford. Place a large sheet of paper on the floor, a table, or a wall. Working in small groups, use different-color markers to draw scribbles all over the paper. Continue drawing until all the children have contributed. When the scribbles are complete, use black and red markers to hide the little mouse and his red knapsack in the drawing, then have the children search for the mouse. Hang the completed work on a wall and invite parents or another class to find the mouse. Make individual "Where's Mouse?" drawings and bind the completed works together to make a classroom book.

Mouse Maze

Read *Mouse Around* by Pat Schories and *Amazing Mazes* by Rolf Heimann. Construct a mouse maze with paper tubes. Collect and bring paper tubes from paper towels, toilet paper, and gift wrap from home. Tape four sheets of poster board together to make a base. Working in small groups, arrange the different kinds of paper tubes end to end on the poster board base to make a maze with a starting and an ending point. Glue the tubes to the base. Discuss the various ways a mouse could go through the maze.

Mouse Hospital

The bramble hedge was most unkind and scratched their eyes and made them blind. The farmer's wife cut off their tails, and the chemist gave them some Never Too Late to Mend medicine. Set up a mouse hospital with some plush mice and and a plastic medicine jar. Use gauze bandages or strips torn from an old sheet to wrap up the injured mice. Be sure to apply some Never Too Late to Mend.

ART/WRITING EXPERIENCE

Watercolor Paintings

Read *Bonjour, Mr. Satie* by Tomie dePaola. Be an artist and paint a picture like Mr. Satie, Rosalie, and Conrad did in the story. Use large watercolor cakes and big brushes. Write a caption for the painting. Display the paintings on the walls or the bulletin board. Bind the paintings together to make a classroom book.

Mouse Tails

Read *The Silly Tail Book* by Marc Brown. Use markers and crayons to create new tails for the three blind mice. Complete the sentence "Some tails are_____." Bind the mouse tail pictures together to make a book.

Mouse Paint

Read *Mouse Paint* by Ellen Stoll Walsh. Three white mice find three jars of paint: red, blue, and yellow. Practice mixing colors with red, yellow, and blue food coloring. Purchase small squeeze bottles of food coloring. Use clear plastic cups of water. Squeeze small drops of different colors of food coloring into the water. Use a craft stick to stir the water. Combine the colors and discover a new color like the white mice did in the story.

Invisible Picture

Use an unlit candle to draw a picture on a sheet of white paper. The drawing will be invisible. Paint over the picture with a watercolor wash. The invisible picture will show through.

COOKING/MATH EXPERIENCE

Mouse Picnic

Look at *Picnic*, a wordless picture book by Emily Arnold McCully. A family of mice goes on a picnic, and one small mouse gets lost on the way. Pack a picnic basket with food for the mice. Food items may include cheese cubes, nuts, raisins, dry cereal, and popcorn. Picnic either indoors or outside. Place the picnic basket in the snack center for an independent experience.

Mystery Snack

Blindfold the children for a mystery snack. Guess what each snack is by smell and by touch. Snack items may include garlic bread, pickles, grapes, fruit, raisins, cheese cubes, ginger cookies, and peanuts.

Cheese Tasting

Read *Anatole and the Cat* by Eve Titus. Anatole the mouse was the chief taster for a cheese factory in France. After tasting each cheese, he would write a word and draw a picture to describe it. Taste different kinds of cheese. Make signs like Anatole's to describe the different tastes. Graph each child's response on a simple bar graph and compare the results.

Mouse Trail Mix

Make a mouse trail mix. Each child can bring one trail mix ingredient from home. Trail mix may include popcorn, dry cereal, pretzels, raisins, nuts, and corn chips. Combine the ingredients in a large bowl. Place the mouse trail mix in the snack center. Use a small scoop to pour trail mix into a small paper cup for an independent snack experience.

From *Story Play*, copyright 1992. Libraries Unlimited/Teacher Ideas Press, P.O. Box 6633, Englewood, CO 80155-6633.

Mouse Jam

In Victoria Chess's illustrations of *Three Blind Mice*, the mice set up a strawberry jam shop. Cook mouse jam for a tasty snack.

combine: 1 quart strawberries

4 cups sugar

Cook over low heat in a large pot, stirring occasionally with a wooden spoon. Bring to a low boil and cook for 15 more minutes. Allow berries to cool and sprinkle with the juice of one-half lemon. For an independent snack activity, use mouse jam with the rebus recipe chart. (See figure 8.6.)

Ten Little Mice

Read *Ten Little Mice* by Joyce Dunbar. Cut a mouse shape from a sponge or sponge sheet. (See figure 8.7.) Sponge-paint mice on a sheet of paper. Count the mice and write the number on the paper.

Fig. 8.6. Mouse jam snack.

1 slice
wheat bread

1 tablespoon
mouse jam

spread jam
on bread

enjoy

Fig. 8.7. Mouse sponge-stamp pattern.

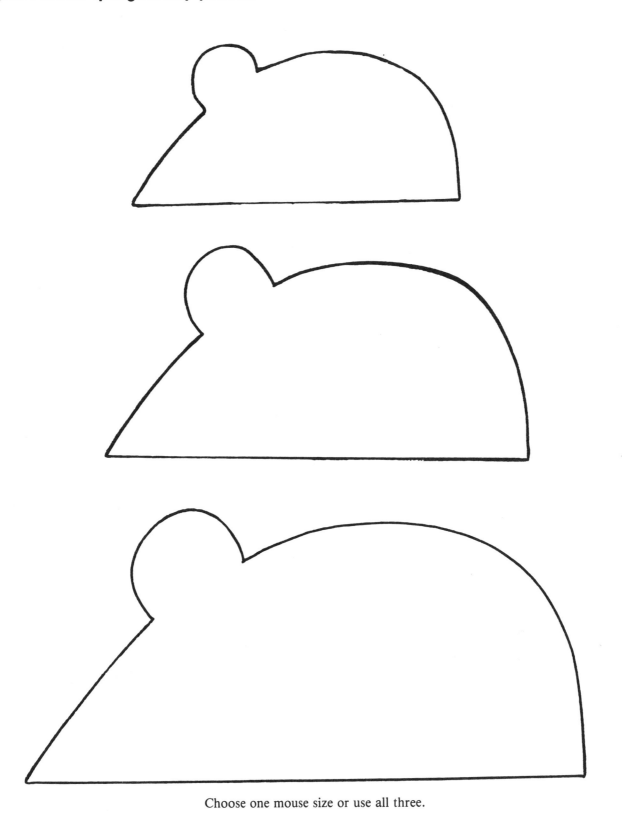

Choose one mouse size or use all three.

SCIENCE/DISCOVERY EXPERIENCE

Mouse Facts

The word *mouse* comes from a Sanskrit word meaning *thief*. Mice are small, with soft fur, pointed snouts, beady black eyes, and thin tails. They belong to the order of mammals called rodents. Mice are gnawing animals with sharp front teeth. They build nests to live in. Newborn mice have pink skin and no fur. Their eyes are closed and they are completely helpless. Mice can hear well, but they have poor eyesight. Some mice are raised for pets.

Mouse Walk

Read *The Listening Walk* by Paul Showers. Take a mouse walk outside and discover a world full of interesting sounds in the everyday environment. On a mouse walk you do not talk, you just listen to the sounds around you. Walk awhile and then stop to listen. The mouse walk can take place indoors as well. Close your eyes and listen to the sounds in the classroom as you walk.

Mice Pets

Visit a pet store and observe pet mice. Purchase a mouse for a classroom pet.

Ear Cones

Make ear cones from paper cups. Cut out the bottoms of the cups and place the large ends over your ears. Play music and hear it get louder or softer as you cover and uncover your ears with the ear cones. Wear the ear cones on the mouse walk.

Matching Textures

Glue materials with different textures onto tagboard cards. Use scraps of rough, smooth, fuzzy, and furry material. Make two cards for each texture. Wear a blindfold and match the textures by touch only.

Rock Crystals

Be a chemist like the one in Victoria Chess's version of *Three Blind Mice*. Make rock crystals from chemical compounds and watch them grow (see fig. 8.8).

Fig. 8.8. Rock crystals.

Materials:	**What to Do:**
Glass bowl	Fill a glass bowl half-full with warm water.
Warm water	
Salt (3 tbls.)	Dissolve the salt in the warm water.
Vinegar (1 tbls.)	
Charcoal briquettes	Add a tablespoon of vinegar.
Magnifying glass	
	Add a layer of charcoal to the bottom of the bowl.
	Set the bowl aside for a few days until the water starts to evaporate.
	Examine the charcoal with a magnifying glass for the formation of rock crystals.

MUSIC/POETRY/GAME EXPERIENCE

Blind Mice Bluff

Play Blind Mice Bluff by forming a circle around three blindfolded "mice." The three blindfolded mice try to guess other players' identities by touching and feeling their hair and faces. Change places and continue until all children have had turns at being mice.

This game may be accompanied by "Blind Mice Bluff," performed by Pamela Copus, or other music. (See bibliography, page 157.)

Squeak-a-Lot

Read *Squeak-a-Lot* by Martin Waddell. A small mouse searches for a friend to play with and learns a lot of games along the way. Pretend to be mice and play the games that are described in the story.

Blind Mice Rope Walk

Remove your shoes and wear a blindfold over your eyes. Lay a rope on the floor in a straight line or a zig-zag pattern. Walk on the rope by feeling it with your feet. The rope walk may be accompanied by Copus's "Blind Mice Bluff."

Mice Choral Reading

Recite the following nursery rhymes for a choral reading.

"Hickory Dickory Dock"

Hickory Dickory, Dock!

The mouse ran up the clock.

The clock struck one,

The mouse ran down.

Hickory, dickory, dock!

"Six Little Mice"

Six little mice sat down to spin;

Pussy passed by and she peeped in.

What are you doing, my little men?

Weaving coats for gentlemen.

Shall I come in and cut off your threads?

No, no, Mistress Pussy, you'd bite off our heads.

Oh, no, I'll not; I'll help you to spin.

That may be so, but you don't come in.

BIBLIOGRAPHY

Three Blind Mice

Ivimey, John W. *Three Blind Mice.* Illustrated by Lorinda Bryan Cauley. New York: G. P. Putnam's Sons, 1991.

Three small mice in search of fun become hungry, scared, blind, wise, and finally happy. After these experiences they settle down and open a pastry shop.

_____.*Three Blind Mice.* Illustrated by Victoria Chess. Boston: Little, Brown & Company, 1990.

The complete story of the three small mice who become blind and what happened afterward. The illustrator's version of the happy ending has the mice opening a jam shop.

_____. *Three Blind Mice.* Illustrated by Paul Galdone. New York: Clarion Books, 1987.

The story is based on the original Mother Goose rhyme by turn-of-the-century writer John W. Ivimey. The illustrator's version of the happy ending has the mice building a house together.

Other Books

Brown, Marc. *The Silly Tail Book*. New York: Parents Magazine Press, 1983.
A short poem describing what tails are and aren't, what they can do and can't, and where they grow and don't.

Cartlidge, Michelle. *A Mouse's Diary*. New York: Lothrop, Lee & Shepard Books, 1981.
A young mouse writes about her ballet class, a shopping trip, a party, and other events in her life.

dePaola, Tomie. *Bonjour, Mr. Satie*. New York: G. P. Putnam's Sons, 1991.
Through the diplomatic efforts of Uncle Satie, two talented Parisian artists end their feud.

_____. *Tomie dePaola's Mother Goose*. New York: G. P. Putnam's Sons, 1985.
An illustrated collection of over 200 nursery rhymes, including "Three Blind Mice."

Dominquez, Angel. *Diary of a Victorian Mouse*. Boston: Little, Brown & Company, 1991.
The diary of a country mouse is discovered in the attic of an old house.

Dunbar, Joyce. *Ten Little Mice*. San Diego, CA: Harcourt Brace Jovanovich, 1990.
The story follows the activities of ten little mice as, one by one, they scurry home to their nest.

Handford, Martin. *Where's Waldo?* London: Walker Books, 1987.
Waldo hikes around the world, and the reader must find him in the illustrations.

Heimann, Rolf. *Amazing Mazes*. Mahwah, NJ: Watermill Press, 1989.
Mind-bending mazes for ages 6 to 60.

Janovitz, Marilyn. *Hickory Dickory Dock*. New York: Hyperion Books for Children, 1991.
In this illustrated version of the old nursery rhyme, mice scamper around a cat's shop and take his lunch while he is napping.

Kraus, Robert. *Where Are You Going, Little Mouse?* New York: Mulberry Books, 1986.
A little mouse runs away from home to find a "nicer" family, but when darkness comes, he misses his own family and realizes how much he loves them.

McCully, Emily Arnold. *Picnic*. New York: Harper & Row, 1984.
A little mouse gets lost on the way to a family picnic.

Schories, Pat. *Mouse Around*. New York: Farrar, Straus & Giroux, 1991.
A wordless picture book about a little mouse's misadventures.

Showers, Paul. *The Listening Walk*. New York: HarperCollins, 1991.
A little girl and her father take a quiet walk and identify the sounds around them.

Stein, Sara Bonnett. *Mouse*. San Diego, CA: Harcourt Brace Jovanovich, 1985.
A nonfiction book that follows the life cycle of a mouse.

Titus, Eve. *Anatole and the Cat*. New York: Bantam Books, 1990.

Anatole's job as a taster in a cheese factory is endangered by a marauding cat.

Waddell, Martin. *Squeak-a-Lot*. New York: Greenwillow Books, 1991.

A mouse's search for someone to play with introduces him to a variety of animal sounds, not all of which suit him very well.

Walsh, Ellen Stoll. *Mouse Paint*. San Diego, CA: Harcourt Brace Jovanovich, 1989.

Three white mice find jars of red, blue, and yellow paint and explore the world of color.

Music

Copus, Pamela, and Joyce Harlow. "Blind Mice Bluff." *Story Play Music*. Englewood, CO: Teacher Ideas Press, 1992.

THE GINGERBREAD BOY

DRAMA/PLAY EXPERIENCE

Introduce "The Gingerbread Boy" by reading one of the versions. Paul Galdone's version is an excellent one to begin with (see bibliography, page 176, for this and other sources). After reading the story, demonstrate the play props and the simpletees costumes.

Simpletees Costumes

Use simpletees costumes of the gingerbread boy, the little old woman, the little old man, and the fox. (See figures 9.1 and 9.2.)

Play Props

Play props can include a toy oven, a plastic mixing bowl, a wooden spoon, a cookie tray, a rolling pin, an oven mitt, and a small apron. The oven can be made from a cardboard box.

Face Masks

Create face masks of the gingerbread boy, the little old woman, the little old man, and the fox. Use tagboard templates to trace the shapes. (See figures 9.3, 9.4, 9.5, and 9.6.)

Stick Puppets/Paper Bag Theater

Make stick puppets of the gingerbread boy, the little old woman, the little old man, and the fox. (See figure 9.7.) Create a paper bag theater for the stick puppets (see fig. 1.7, on page 8). Present the play to a friend or take home and present to parents.

Fig. 9.1. Simpletees costumes. The Gingerbread Boy.

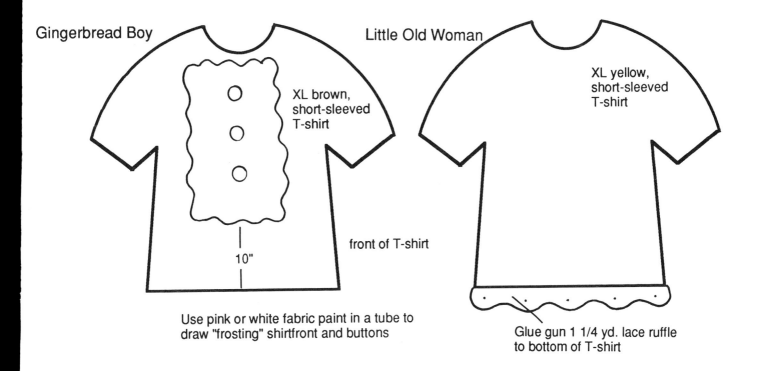

Gingerbread Boy

XL brown,
short-sleeved
T-shirt

front of T-shirt

10"

Use pink or white fabric paint in a tube to
draw "frosting" shirtfront and buttons

Little Old Woman

XL yellow,
short-sleeved
T-shirt

Glue gun 1 1/4 yd. lace ruffle
to bottom of T-shirt

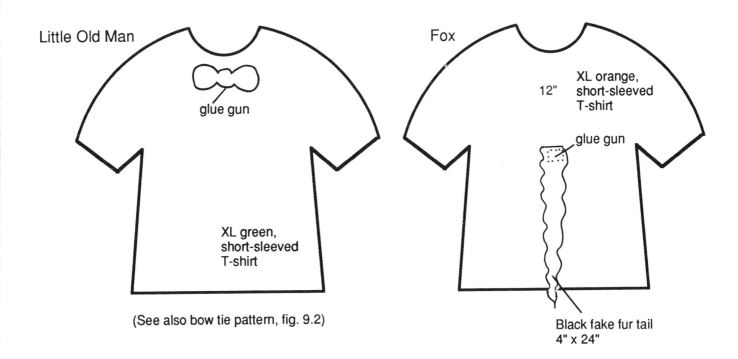

Little Old Man

glue gun

XL green,
short-sleeved
T-shirt

(See also bow tie pattern, fig. 9.2)

Fox

XL orange,
short-sleeved
T-shirt

12"

glue gun

Black fake fur tail
4" x 24"

Fig. 9.2. Little old man bow tie directions and pattern.

Materials:

Yellow craft felt square
Scissors
Glue gun

What to Do:

Use pattern to cut 1 yellow felt bow tie.

Glue the bow tie to the T-shirt.

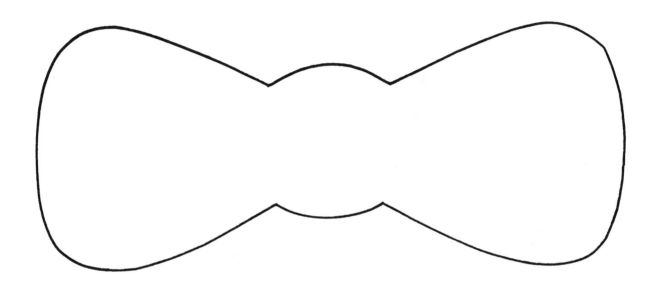

Fig. 9.3. Gingerbread boy face mask pattern.

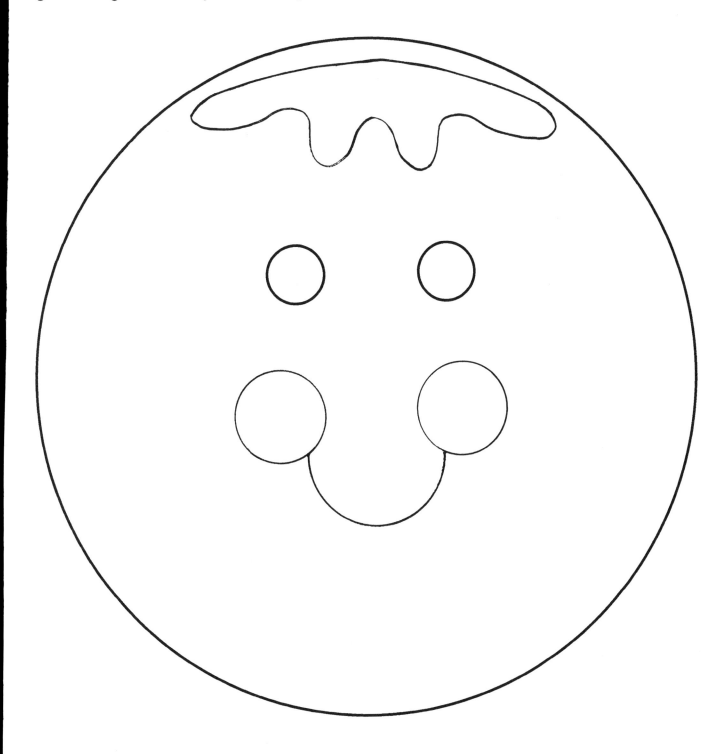

Fig. 9.4. Little old woman face mask pattern.

Fig. 9.5. Little old man face mask pattern.

From *Story Play*, copyright 1992. Libraries Unlimited/Teacher Ideas Press, P.O. Box 6633, Englewood, CO 80155-6633.

Fig. 9.6. Fox face mask pattern.

Fig. 9.7. The Gingerbread Boy stick puppet patterns.

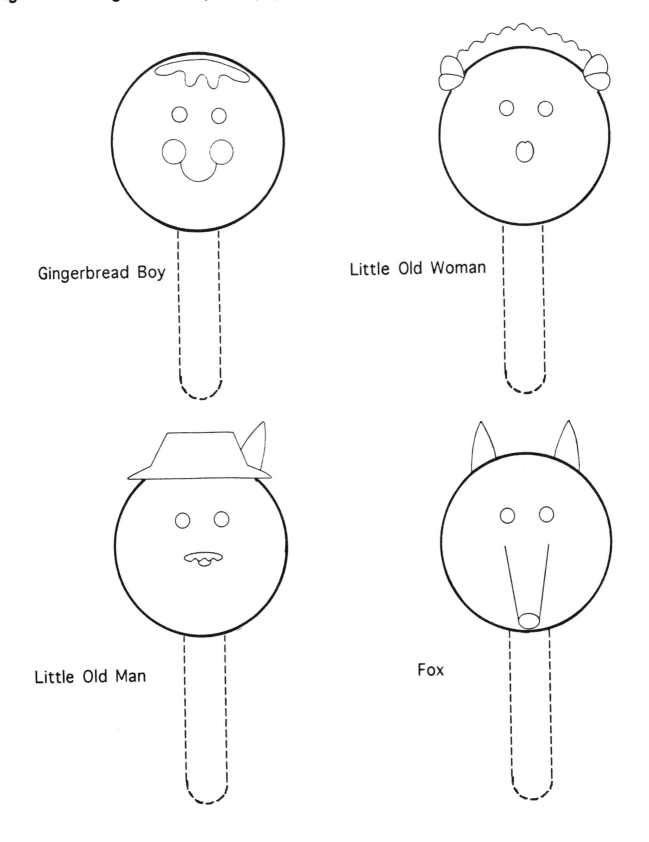

Gingerbread Boy

Little Old Woman

Little Old Man

Fox

LITERATURE/WRITING EXPERIENCE

The Gingerbread Boy *Versions*

Read the different versions of "The Gingerbread Boy." Paul Galdone's version is based on the traditional story, while Lorinda Bryan Cauley's is the retelling of a variant from Norway. *The Fine Round Cake* by Arnica Esterl is a variation of "The Gingergread Boy" adapted from the classic English fairy tale.

The Gingerbread Boy *Children's Version*

After reading different versions of "The Gingerbread Boy," write a children's version on a large sheet of chart paper. Discuss using different characters or a different ending to the story.

Key-Word Books and Key Words

Make a key-word book for the unique and important words in the story. The key words for "The Ginger-bread Boy" are as follows:

gingerbread	boy	woman
man	oven	run
catch	fox	jump
river		

Gingerbread Boy Shape Book

Make a gingerbread boy shape book by tracing the pattern from a tagboard template. (See figure 9.8.) Illustrate and write the story of "The Gingerbread Boy." Use the key words for an independent writing experience.

Birthday Book

The little old woman wanted a child so much that she made a gingerbread boy who came to life. Debra Frasier's *On the Day You Were Born* celebrates the birth of a newborn baby. Write or tell about the day you were born. Make a birthday book and illustrate it. (See figure 9.9.) Rub baby lotion on your hands and arms. Inhale the scent.

Beastly Birthday Book

Read Babette Cole's *Beastly Birthday Book*. Someone is having a birthday, and all his friends are coming, including some singing cows, raging rhinos, and circus sharks. Each guest brings a present. Lift the flaps on each page spread and find the presents tucked inside. Make a beastly birthday book. (See figure 9.10.) Draw birthday presents and tuck them inside the pockets.

Fig. 9.8. Gingerbread boy shape book directions and pattern.

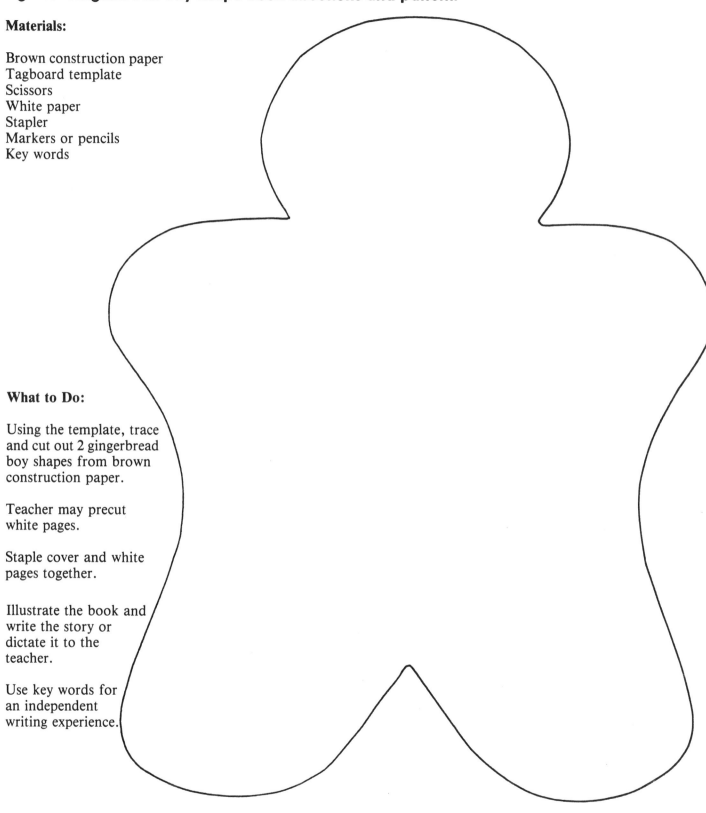

Materials:

Brown construction paper
Tagboard template
Scissors
White paper
Stapler
Markers or pencils
Key words

What to Do:

Using the template, trace
and cut out 2 gingerbread
boy shapes from brown
construction paper.

Teacher may precut
white pages.

Staple cover and white
pages together.

Illustrate the book and
write the story or
dictate it to the
teacher.

Use key words for
an independent
writing experience.

Fig. 9.9. Birthday Book directions and pattern.

Materials:

Pink or blue
    construction paper
Tagboard template
White paper
Markers or pencils
Scissors
Stapler
Key words

What to Do:

Using the tagboard
template, trace and cut
out 2 birthday shapes
from pink or blue con-
struction paper.

Teacher may precut
white pages.

Staple together the
cover and the white
pages.

Illustrate the book and
write the story or dictate
it to the teacher.

Use key words for an
independent writing
experience.

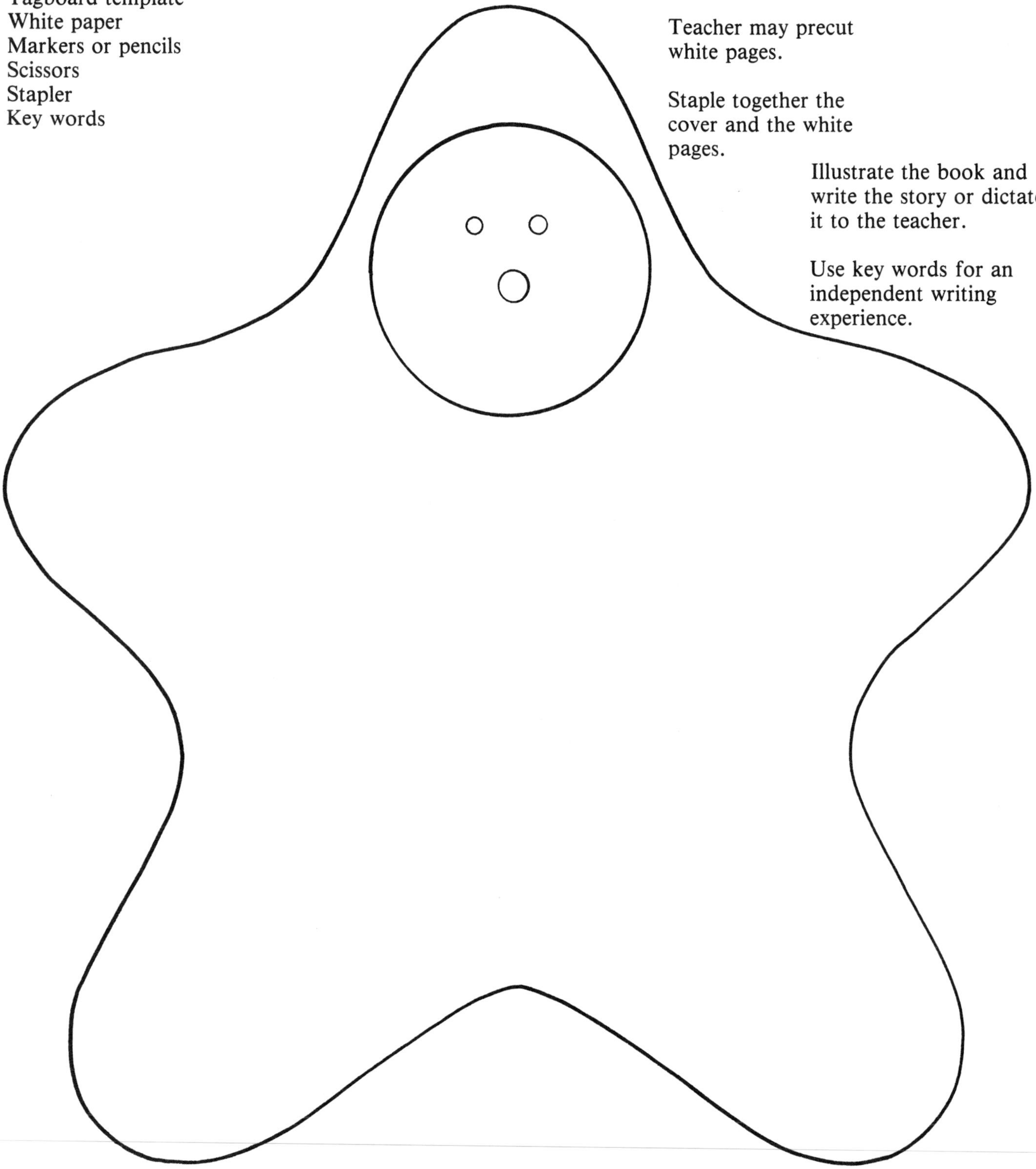

Fig. 9.10. Beastly birthday book.

- Fold pieces of paper in half and glue an envelope to one side of each piece of folded paper.

- Staple the pages together to form a book.

- Trim the glued edge from each envelope flap.

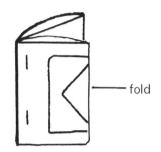

- Draw presents or write notes to go inside the envelopes.

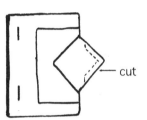

- Illustrate or write on the other sides of the pages who or what might come to the birthday party.

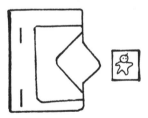

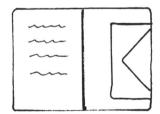

COOPERATIVE/GROUP EXPERIENCE

The Gingerbread Boy Map

Read Gail Hartman's *As the Crow Flies: A First Book of Maps.* Discuss the maps of the different animals' journeys. Read Ronnie Randall's version of *The Gingerbread Man.* Discuss the gingerbread boy's journey in the book. Compare the gingerbread boy's journey to the journeys in Gail Hartman's book. In Randall's version, the gingerbread boy ran across the kitchen, down the road, past a big gray cat sitting on a fence, past a brown dog lying beside a hedge, past a cow in a field, and past a fox sitting under a tree by the river. Working in small groups, make a map of the gingerbread boy's journey. Use a long sheet of brown wrapping paper for the map.

The Gingerbread Trail

Read *The Secret Birthday Message* by Eric Carle. The secret message is written in code, and Tim must decipher it to find his birthday gift. Hide a gingerbread boy in the school and write a secret code using a rebus format. Working in small groups, the children can follow the clues and discover the gingerbread boy's hiding place. Use the same code and hiding place for everyone or prepare different ones for each group.

Birthday Celebration

Read *Dinner with Fox* by Stephen Wyllie. Fox invites his friends to dinner with written invitations. Plan a communal birthday celebration. Make invitations and invite each other or parents to attend the birthday celebration. Ask a parent volunteer to bake a giant cake. Read *The Biggest Birthday Cake in the World* by Elizabeth Spurr. Create party decorations or table centerpieces. Sing "Happy Birthday to Me."

ART/WRITING EXPERIENCE

Tempera Paintings

After reading the different versions of "The Gingerbread Boy," paint a picture about the story. Instead of the traditional brown, choose a different color for the gingerbread boy. Paint a blue or a green gingerbread boy. Write a caption for the picture. Display the paintings on the walls and the bulletin board, or bind the paintings together to make a classroom book.

Finger Painting

Choose a finger paint color and cover a sheet of paper with the paint. Allow the paint to dry. Trace a gingerbread boy or girl shape on the paper and cut it out. (See figures 9.11 and 9.12.) Add features to the gingerbread boy or girl. Create a background and display the gingerbread boys and girls in a group setting. Write a title or caption for the display. Write word balloons for each gingerbread boy and girl.

Fig. 9.11. Gingerbread boy pattern.

Fig. 9.12. Gingerbread girl pattern.

COOKING/MATH EXPERIENCE

Gingerbread Boys and Girls

Prepare gingerbread dough according to the directions on a packaged mix. Roll out the dough on a piece of wax paper. Use a gingerbread boy or girl cookie cutter to cut out the cookies. Bake according to the directions on the box. Decorate with a plastic tube or prepared icing. Ready-to-use icing in plastic tubes can be purchased at the grocery store.

Pancake People

Read *Pancakes, Pancakes!* by Eric Carle. Discuss the sequence of preparing pancakes in the story. Make pancakes and write on a large sheet of chart paper the sequence of events as they happen. List the utensils and the ingredients. Mix the pancake batter according to the directions. Preheat an electric skillet and melt some butter in it. Drop the pancake batter by the tablespoonful into the heated butter, making small, round cakes. Make a face on each pancake with the raisins from the science/discovery experience (see page 175). Flip the pancakes over and cook the other side. Remove the pancakes and place them on a paper towel or a small paper plate. Allow the pancakes to cool slightly.

Cinnamon Person

Make a cinnamon person from a rebus recipe. (See figure 9.13.) On a piece of wax paper, roll one refrigerator biscuit into a long snake. Make a cinnamon person by pinching the "snake" into segments for the head, arms, and legs. Sprinkle the person with a mixture of cinnamon and sugar. Bake as directed on the biscuit can.

From *Story Play*, copyright 1992. Libraries Unlimited/Teacher Ideas Press, P.O. Box 6633, Englewood, CO 80155-6633.

Fig. 9.13. Cinnamon Person.

1 biscuit

roll "snake"

shape person

sprinkle with
cinnamon/sugar

bake and eat

SCIENCE/DISCOVERY EXPERIENCE

Spice Facts

The word *spice* comes from the French word *epice*. This, in turn, comes from the Latin word *species*, which means *sort* or *kind*. The word *specie* also means *money*. Spices have been used as money and as gifts in the past. The Moluccas, or Spice Islands, are primarily in the eastern part of Indonesia, the most famous source of spices. Early explorers discovered the spices that grow on the islands and introduced them to European markets. Spices are used to flavor some foods. Spices have sharp tastes and odors. Some herbs, such as sage, marjoram, thyme, and rosemary, can be grown in a kitchen window.

Spice Samplers

Use 4-by-4-inch cards for spice samples. Paint a circle of glue in the middle of each card. Sprinkle a different spice or herb into the glue on each card. Spices and herbs can include allspice, cinnamon, cloves, ginger, marjoram, mustard, nutmeg, paprika, pepper, rosemary, sage, and thyme. Label each card with the name of the spice or herb.

Grapes to Raisins

Purchase some seedless grapes. Wash the grapes and remove them from the stems. Put the grapes on a paper plate and place them in the sun. Allow the grapes to dry out and become raisins. Use the raisins to decorate the gingerbread and pancake people for the cooking/math experience. (See page 173).

Ginger to Cake

Read Rose Robart's *The Cake That Mack Ate*. The story begins, "This : the cake that Mack ate. This is the egg that went into the cake that Mack ate." Brainstorm about how a ginger or spice cake is made. Write the ideas on a large sheet of chart paper and number them in a possible chronological order. Bake a ginger or spice cake from scratch.

MUSIC/POETRY/GAME EXPERIENCE

The Birthday

Read *Birthday Presents* by Cynthia Rylant. The story follows a child from her day of birth through five birthday celebrations to the present. What does the word *birthday* mean? Make life-size puppets by tracing outlines of each other on brown wrapping paper. Attach the paper arms and legs to your arms and legs with rubber bands.

The children may listen to "The Birth Day," performed by Pamela Copus, as an additional activity. (See bibliography, page 178.) Listen to the music, and curl into a small ball, then uncurl as if you were being born.

Flee the Fox

Place two pieces of rope or string in parallel lines about a foot apart. Jump back and forth across the river to escape the fox. Widen the river to make crossing it more difficult. Choose someone to be the fox and chase the gingerbread boys and girls back and forth across the river.

Pancake Man

Recite the "Pancake Man" together:

Pancake man, pancake man,

Bake me a cake as fast as you can.

Put him in the oven and shut the door.

When he's done I'll cry more, more, more.

Pancake man, pancake man,

Bake me a cake as fast as you can.

Write the poem on a large sheet of chart paper. Clap your hands and then your thighs to keep time with the rhythm of the poem.

BIBLIOGRAPHY

The Gingerbread Boy Versions

Cauley, Lorinda Bryan. *The Pancake Boy.* New York: G. P. Putnam's Sons, 1985.
   A pancake boy runs away from the little old woman who made him. A variant of a classic folktale from Norway.

Esterl, Arnica. *The Fine Round Cake.* New York: Macmillan, 1991.
   A variation of the gingerbread boy story, adapted from a classic English fairy tale.

Galdone, Paul. *The Gingerbread Boy.* New York: Clarion Books, 1975.
   The gingerbread boy eludes the hungry grasp of everyone he meets, until he happens upon a fox who is more clever than he.

Jacobs, Joseph. "Johnny Cake." In *Favorite Fairy Tales*, by Tomie dePaola. New York: G. P. Putnam's Sons, 1986.

Randall, Ronnie. *The Gingerbread Man.* Lewistown, ME: Ladybird Books, 1987.

Other Books

Asch, Frank. *Happy Birthday, Moon.* New York: Simon & Schuster, 1982.
When a bear discovers that the moon shares his birthday, he buys the moon a beautiful hat as a present.

Bunting, Eve. *Happy Birthday, Dear Duck.* New York: Clarion Books, 1988.
Duck's birthday gifts from his animal friends are wonderful but cannot be used away from the water, a problem solved by the arrival of his last gift.

Carle, Eric. *Pancakes, Pancakes!* Saxonville, MA: Picture Book Studio, 1990.
By cutting and grinding the wheat for flour, Jack starts from scratch to help make his breakfast pancake.

_____. *The Secret Birthday Message.* New York: HarperCollins, 1971.
A message in code starts Tim off on an exciting treasure hunt, until at the end he finds a happy surprise.

Cole, Babette. *Beastly Birthday Book.* New York: Doubleday, 1991.
Someone is having a birthday party. Lift the flaps and find the birthday presents tucked inside.

Frasier, Debra. *On the Day You Were Born.* San Diego, CA: Harcourt Brace Jovanovich, 1991.
The earth celebrates the birth of a newborn baby.

Hartman, Gail. *As the Crow Flies: A First Book of Maps.* New York: Bradbury Press, 1990.
A look at different geographical areas from the perspectives of an eagle, a rabbit, a crow, a horse, and a gull.

Hoban, Russell. *A Birthday for Francis.* New York: HarperCollins, 1968.
It is Gloria's birthday. Francis doesn't know whether she should be happy for her little sister or sad for herself.

Robart, Rose. *The Cake That Mack Ate.* Boston: Little, Brown & Co., 1986.
A cumulative tale about the making of a birthday cake from start to finish.

Rylant, Cynthia. *Birthday Presents.* New York: Orchard Books, 1987.
A five-year-old girl listens to her parents describe her four previous birthday celebrations.

Sawyer, Ruth. *Journey Cake, Ho!* Middlesex, England: Puffin Books, 1953.
Johnny is leaving the farm because of hard times. His journey cake leads him on a merry chase that results in a farmyard full of animals and the family being all together again.

Spurr, Elizabeth. *The Biggest Birthday Cake in the World.* San Diego, CA: Harcourt Brace Jovanovich, 1991.
The richest and fattest man in the world wishes for the biggest birthday cake in the world, and on his birthday discovers the joy of sharing.

Stock, Catherine. *Birthday Present.* New York: Bradbury Press, 1991.
Although he is not pleased with his mother's choice of a gift for him to take to a birthday party, a little boy attends and discovers a pleasant surprise.

Wyllie, Stephen. *Dinner with Fox.* New York: Dial Books for Young Readers, 1990.

   Fox invites his friends to dinner and grows plumper each day, until an unexpected guest demands a change in the menu.

Music

Copus, Pamela, and Joyce Harlow. "The Birth Day." *Story Play Music.* Englewood, CO: Teacher Ideas Press, 1992.

THREE LITTLE KITTENS

DRAMA/PLAY EXPERIENCE

Introduce the "Three Little Kittens" by reading the nursery rhyme, then introduce the simpletees costume and the play props.

Simpletees Costumes

Use simpletees costumes of the three kittens and the mother cat. (See figure 10.1.) For cat ears pattern, see figure 4.17 on page 79.

Play Props

Play props can include a small table, chairs, a tea set, a small clothes rack, clothespins, three sets of mittens, and a dishpan in which to wash the mittens.

Face Masks

Create face masks of the three kittens and the mother cat. Using tagboard templates, trace and cut out the masks. (See figures 10.2 and 10.3.)

Stick Puppets/Paper Bag Theater

Make stick puppets of the three kittens and the mother cat. (See figure 10.4.) Create a paper bag theater for the stick puppets. (See figure 1.7 on page 8.) Present the "Three Little Kittens" to a friend or take home and present to parents.

Fig. 10.1. Simpletees costumes: Three Little Kittens.

Kittens (make 3)

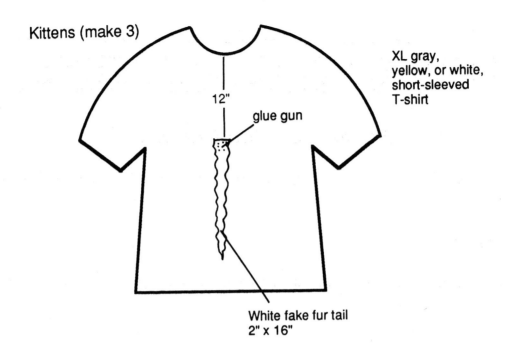

12"

glue gun

XL gray,
yellow, or white,
short-sleeved
T-shirt

White fake fur tail
2" x 16"

Mother Cat

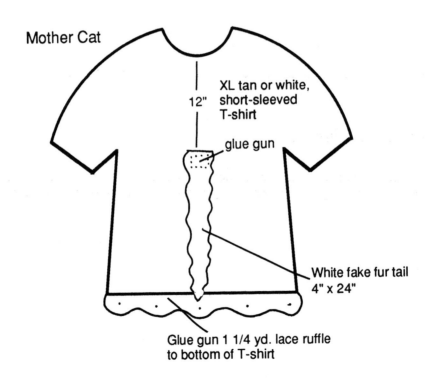

XL tan or white,
short-sleeved
T-shirt

12"

glue gun

White fake fur tail
4" x 24"

Glue gun 1 1/4 yd. lace ruffle
to bottom of T-shirt

Fig. 10.2. Kittens face mask pattern.

Fig. 10.3. Mother cat face mask pattern.

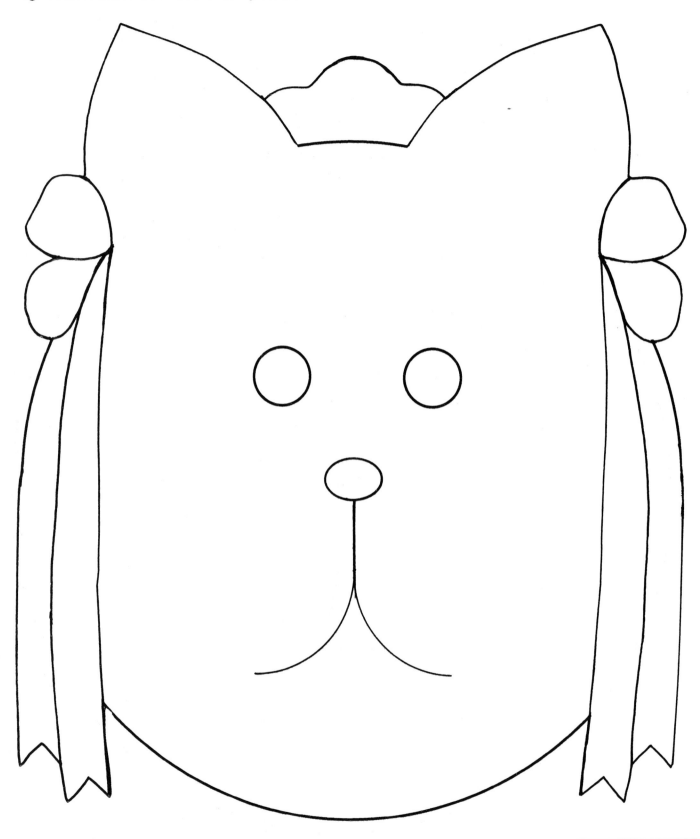

Fig. 10.4. Three Little Kittens stick puppet patterns.

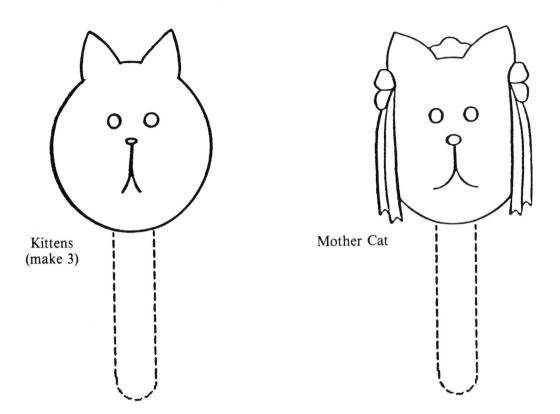

Kittens
(make 3)

Mother Cat

LITERATURE/WRITING EXPERIENCE

Three Little Kittens *Nursery Rhyme*

Read the "Three Little Kittens" nursery rhyme. (See bibliography, page 192, for a list of sources.) Discuss the sequence of events in the story. For example, what happened when the kittens lost their mittens? What happened when they found their mittens? Explore and discuss cause and effect relationships.

Key-Word Books and Key Words

Make a key-word book using the unique or important words in the story. The key words for "Three Little Kittens" are the following:

kittens	mittens	pie
cry	sigh	dry
dear	fear	soiled
washed		

Kitten Shape Book

Make a kitten shape book from a tagboard template. (See figure 10.5.) Illustrate the book and write the story or dictate it to the teacher. Use the key words for an independent writing experience.

Meow

Read *Meow* by Bernie Karlin. *Meow* is the only word used throughout the book. The illustrations demonstrate what each *meow* means. Use markers to draw a picture of a cat. Use a word balloon and the word *meow*. Bind the drawings together to make a meow book for the classroom.

I Want a _____

Read *I Want a Cat* by Tony Ross. When a little girl cannot have the cat she wants, she makes a cat suit and becomes a cat. Discuss the pet you would like to have. Pretend to become that pet. Use markers to draw the pet. Complete the sentence "I want a _____." Bind the illustrations together to make a classroom book.

Fig. 10.5. Kitten shape book directions and patterns.

Materials:

Yellow construction paper
Tagboard template
White paper
Scissors
Stapler
Markers or pencils
Key words

What to Do:

Using tagboard and template trace and cut out 2 kitten shapes from yellow construction paper.

Teacher may precut white pages.

Staple the cover and pages together.

Illustrate the book and write or dictate the story.

Use key words for an independent writing experience.

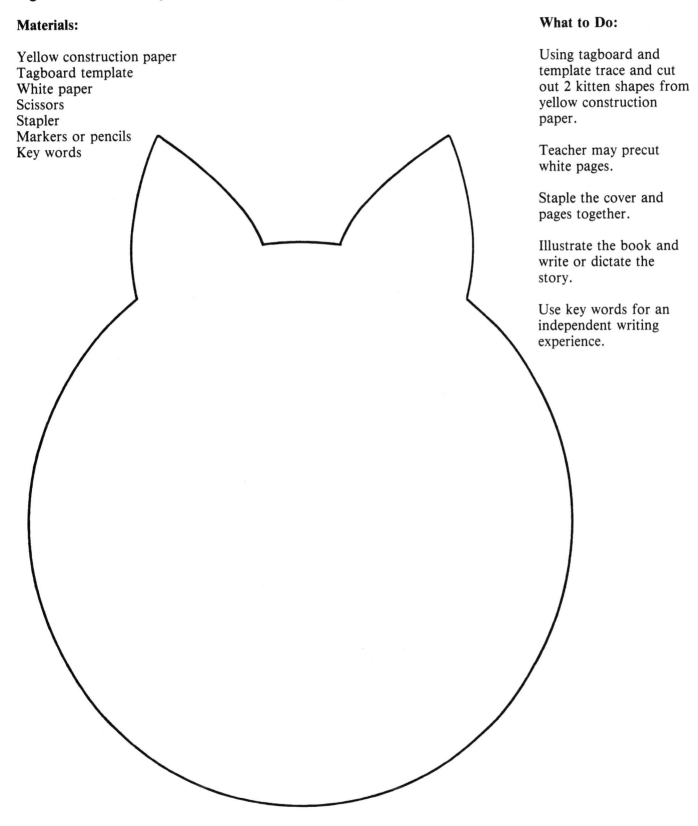

COOPERATIVE/GROUP EXPERIENCE

Dreamscape

Read Lane Smith's *The Big Pets.* "The girl was small and the cat was big." So begins the story of the night children and their dreamscape, where all the children are small and their pets are big. Paint a dreamscape. Use blue tempera as the base color. Add different amounts of black and red to the base color to create an array of different night shades. Working in small groups, paint the dreamscape on a large sheet of mural paper. Allow the dreamscape to dry overnight.

Big Pets

Working in small groups, design an imaginary big pet. Use a large sheet of paper and big watercolor markers. Discuss how the pet can be shared by its creators. Take turns letting the pet spend the night. Bring the pet back to school and tell what took place during the overnight visit.

ART/WRITING EXPERIENCE

Watercolor Paintings

Read *The Picture Book of Cats* by Yoko Imoto. Discuss the softness of the watercolor paintings of the cats. Paint a picture of the three kittens using yellow, brown, black, and red watercolors. Write captions for the paintings and display them on the walls or the bulletin board. Bind the paintings together to make a classroom book.

_____'s Special Room

Read *Alice's Special Room* by Dick Gackenbach. Alice has a special room where she can play with her cat who has died. Fold a sheet of construction paper in half. Use watercolor markers to draw a special room on the inside page. Cut a door on the outside page for entering the special room. Discuss or write about the room and what takes place inside it.

Mitten Pocket

Read Jan Brett's *The Mitten.* Design a mitten pocket. (See figure 10.6.) Use markers to draw different animals. Cut out the animals and place them inside the mitten pocket.

Fig. 10.6. Mitten pocket directions and pattern.

Materials:

White construction paper
Tagboard template
White paper
Scissors
Stapler
Markers or pencils
Key words

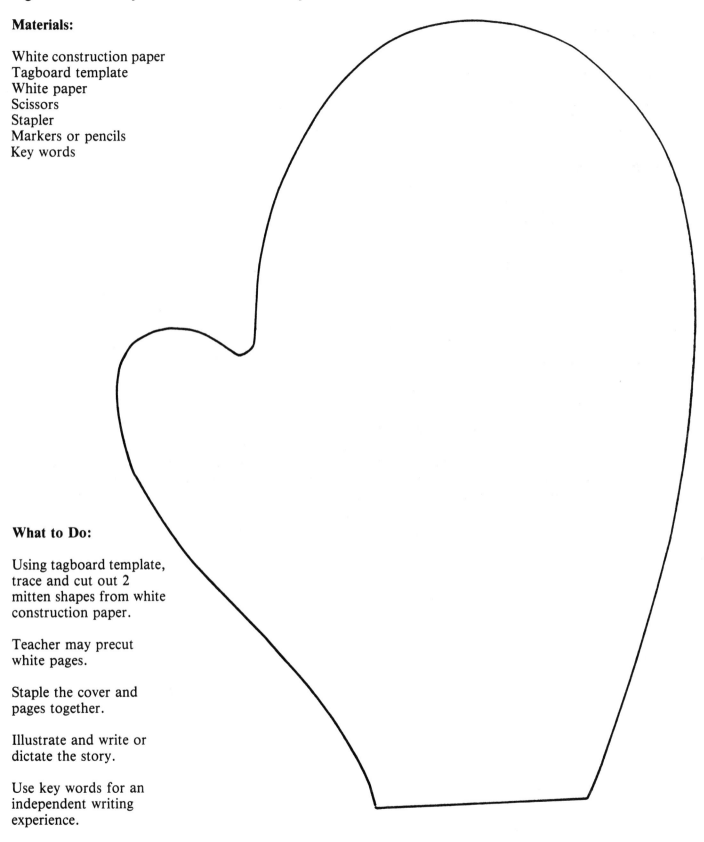

What to Do:

Using tagboard template, trace and cut out 2 mitten shapes from white construction paper.

Teacher may precut white pages.

Staple the cover and pages together.

Illustrate and write or dictate the story.

Use key words for an independent writing experience.

COOKING/MATH EXPERIENCE

A Pair of Pairs

Read the book *One, Two, One Pair!* by Bruce McMillan. After seeing the different pairs of things in the book, bring a pair of things from home. Discuss and display the sets of pairs. Pick a partner for the day. Spend the day doing everything in pairs. For example, pair up to go outside or to lunch. Work and play together in pairs.

Matching Mittens

Sort a collection of real mittens into pairs. Use clothespins to hang the pairs of mittens together on a clothesline or a small drying rack.

Kitten Pie

Make kitten pie. Follow the rebus recipe for an independent experience. (See figure 10.7.) Purchase a can of large flaky biscuits and a can of cherry pie filling. Separate a biscuit into two layers. Place a teaspoon of pie filling on one of the layers. Put the other layer on top of the cherry pie filling. Use a fork to crimp the edges of the biscuit together. Bake according to the directions on the can. Let the kitten pie cool and then eat it.

Cats Everywhere

Read *A House Full of Cats* by Kitty Higgins. Miss Durbin and her dog share their house with 204 cats. The teacher can cut a cat shape from a sponge or compressed sponge sheet. (See figure 10.8.) Spread tempera on a flat tray. Dip the cat-shaped sponge into the tempera and then stamp cat shapes on a piece of paper. Count the cats and write the number on the paper.

Fig. 10.7. Kitten pie.

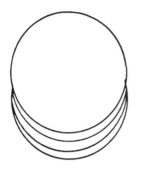

separate
flaky biscuit

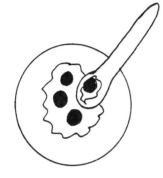

spread cherry
pie filling

put on top
half of biscuit

crimp edges

bake and eat

Fig. 10.8. Cat sponge-stamp pattern.

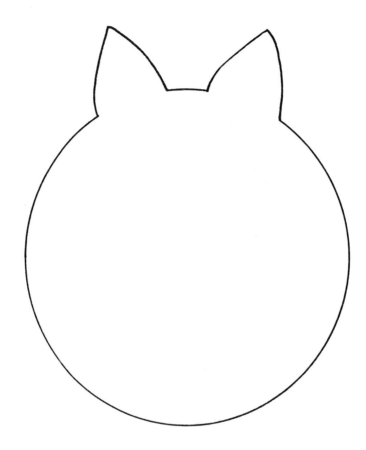

SCIENCE/DISCOVERY EXPERIENCE

Cat Facts

Read *Amazing Cats* by Dorothy Kindersley and *Kitten* by Jan Burton. Cats make wonderful pets. Some have long fur, while others have short fur. Cats are clever hunters. They kill rats and mice for farmers. Cats eat meat. Their sharp teeth and claws help them tear the meat apart. Their claws help them climb trees, to find food, and to escape from an enemy. Cats purr when they are happy and hiss when they are angry. They arch their backs and puff up their fur when angry or frightened. The Egyptians were probably the first people to tame cats. They made their deceased cats into mummies and buried them with their masters or in cat cemeteries.

Cat Mummies

Read *The Kids' Cat Book* by Tomie dePaola. The book shows how mummies were made and why the Egyptians made mummies of their cats. Bring stuffed cats from home. Using gauze bandages, wrap the cats to make mummies.

MUSIC/POETRY/GAME EXPERIENCE

Here Sit the Kittens

Choose three children to be the kittens. The kittens sit in three chairs with their backs to the class. Place a mitten under each chair. Select three children to steal the mittens from under the chairs. The kittens must guess who stole their mittens. The thieves then become the kittens, and the game is repeated until all have participated.

The above game may be accompanied by "Here Sit the Kittens," performed by Pamela Copus. (See bibliography, page 193.) Alternatively, the class may recite "Here Sit the Kittens" as the mittens are "stolen."

Here sit the kittens in the chair, chair, chair.

They lost their mittens, they don't care, care, care.

Can they find their mittens, oh where, where, where?

Did you hide their mittens, did you dare, dare, dare?

Copycat

Play copycat. Pick a partner and face each other. One partner copies everything the other partner does, then the partners reverse roles. Change partners and repeat the process. You can play copycat either indoors or outside.

The Mitten Song

Recite "The Mitten Song."

Thumbs in the thumb place,

Fingers all together.

This is the song

We sing in mitten weather.

When it is cold,

It doesn't matter whether

Mittens are wool

Or made of finest leather.

This is the song

We sing in mitten weather—

Thumbs in the thumb place,

Fingers all together.

BIBLIOGRAPHY

Three Little Kittens *Versions*

Cauley, Lorinda Bryan. *The Three Little Kittens*. New York: G. P. Putnam's Sons, 1982.

Galdone, Paul. *Three Little Kittens*. New York: Clarion Books, 1986.

dePaola, Tomie. "Three Little Kittens." In *Tomie dePaola's Mother Goose*. New York: G. P. Putnam's Sons, 1985.

Lobel, Arnold. "Three Little Kittens." In *The Random House Book of Mother Goose: A Treasury of 306 Timeless Nursery Rhymes*. New York: Random House, 1986.

Lucas, Barbara. *Cats by Mother Goose*. New York: Lothrop, Lee & Shepard Books, 1986.

Obligado, Lillian. *The Three Little Kittens*. New York: Random House, 1974.

Other Books

Brett, Jan. *The Mitten*. New York: G. P. Putnam's Sons, 1989.
    A Ukrainian folktale about a boy who loses his white mitten in the snow. He can't find his mitten but a lot of animals do.

Burton, Jane. *Kitten*. New York: Dutton Children's Books, 1991.
    Photographs and text follow a kitten from birth to 10 weeks old.

dePaola, Tomie. *The Kids' Cat Book*. New York: Holiday House, 1979.
    Patrick learns everything there is to know about cats and their place in art and literature.

Gackenbach, Dick. *Alice's Special Room*. New York: Clarion Books, 1991.
    Alice has a special room where she goes to play with her cat who died a year ago.

Higgins, Kitty. *A House Full of Cats*. Los Angeles: Price/Stern/Sloan, 1991.
    Miss Durbin must share her house with 1 dog and 204 cats, which fill all of her living space.

Imoto, Yoko. *The Picture Book of Cats*. Tokyo: Kodansha, 1984.
    A beautiful picture book of cats and kittens with all their irresistible charm.

Karlin, Bernie. *Meow*. New York: Simon & Schuster, 1991.
    A cat's constant meowing annoys everyone until they learn the reason for all the noise.

McMillan, Bruce. *One, Two, One Pair!* New York: Scholastic, 1991.
    Photographs illustrate the concept of pairs.

Parsons, Alexandra. *Amazing Cats*. New York: Alfred A. Knopf, 1990.
    Photographs give a close-up look at some of the world's most amazing cats.

Ross, Tony. *I Want a Cat*. New York: Farrar, Straus & Giroux, 1989.
  Jessy wanted a cat. When she couldn't have one, she decided to become one.

Smith, Lane. *The Big Pets*. New York: Viking Penguin, 1991.
  A little girl explores a dreamscape with her big pet and meets the other night children and their pets.

Music

Copus, Pamela, and Joyce Harlow. "Here Sit the Kittens." *Story Play Music*. Englewood, CO: Teacher Ideas Press, 1992.

INDEX

ABOUT THE AUTHOR

Joyce Harlow was born into a family of eight children. With her brothers and sisters for playmates, she spent her childhood exploring the woods and creeks on her grandfather's farm. Her earliest years were spent in countless hours of creative and imaginative play. Following the example of her brothers and sisters, she became an avid reader at an early age. Fairy tales played an important role in her earliest exposure to reading. Becoming a teacher of young children allowed her love of reading, creativity, and imaginative play to continue. *Story Play* is the result of teaching kindergarten at Summerfield Academy in Spring, Texas. Joyce Harlow conducts workshops and teacher in-service training based on the concepts from the book.